G000153313

The Scriptures clearly teach the ir thinking rightly. Many of the p: about God, and Paul instructed th to seek the things above and set their minds on things above. And to the Philippians Paul wrote, 'whatever is true, honorable, just, pure, lovely, of moral excellence and praiseworthy, think about these things.' Only God truly fits this description. It is for these reasons *I AM: A Biblical and Devotional Study of the Attributes of God* is such a gift to the Church. In a clear, accessible way Brian A. Russell has provided a wonderful resource for believers today not only to understand God's revelation of Himself but to recognize the significance and relevance of God's attributes to believers in their everyday walk of life.

T. J. Betts
Professor of Old Testament Interpretation, Southern Baptist
Theological Seminary, Louisville, Kentucky

There is no subject more worthy of our attention or more stretching to our finite minds than the infinite, eternal and unchangeable being and character of God. Brian A. Russell presents the teaching of Scripture and distills some of the best insights of those in the history of the church who have thought about God's revelation of himself in Scripture, clearly explaining and warmly applying the key attributes of our great Triune God. For anyone who wants to know God better, this is a book that will deepen their understanding and move their hearts to love and worship.

Warren Peel
Minister of Trinity Reformed Presbyterian Church,
Professor of New Testament Language and Literature,
Reformed Theological College, Belfast

Brian A. Russell has given us a perceptive and thoroughly biblical exploration of the attributes of God. As they make their way through this profound yet understandable study, the reader will surely grow in their knowledge of God's infinite greatness and increase their love for Him.

Rebecca Stark
Blogger at Rebecca Writes, Revive our Hearts and Out of the Ordinary,
Author of *The Good Portion: God*

Ah! The vision of God: the height of human endeavour! Seeing Him more clearly, loving Him more dearly, and following Him more nearly. Such are the goals of a God-centred life, and are the major theme of Brian Russell's theological and devotional focus. Allow your mind to be stretched and your heart warmed!

Simon Vibert,
Vicar of Christ Church, Virginia Water,
Author of several books, including *The Perpetual Battle: The World, the Flesh, and the Devil*

I AM

A devotional study of the attributes of God

BRIAN A. RUSSELL

Grace
Publications

CHRISTIAN
FOCUS

Copyright © Brian A. Russell 2019

paperback ISBN 978-1-5271-0364-1
epub ISBN 978-1-5271-0459-4
mobi ISBN 978-1-5271-0460-0

Published in 2019
by
Christian Focus Publications Ltd,
Geanies House, Fearn, Ross-shire, IV20 1TW, Scotland
www.christianfocus.com
and
Grace Publications Trust
7 Arlington Way London EC1R 1XA
e-mail: editors@gracepublications.co.uk
www.gracepublications.co.uk

A CIP catalogue record for this book is available
from the British Library.

Cover design by Tom Barnard

Printed and bound by
Bell and Bain, Glasgow

CONTENTS

CONTENTS

Dedicated to:

Pastors and Bible College students in the Third World
who do not have the means to purchase Christian
books which 'contend earnestly for the faith
which was once for all delivered to the saints.'
(Jude 6)

ACKNOWLEDGMENTS

I am deeply indebted to:

Grace Publications Trust for their help in publishing my books over nineteen years and helping to distribute them freely through Grace Baptist Mission to pastors and Bible College students in Third World countries – a ministry dear to my heart;

The editorial staff of Grace Publications Trust and Christian Focus for their help in preparing the manuscript for publication;

My wife Muriel, who has been a constant source of encouragement and tireless helper for the past sixty years.

SOLI DEO GLORIA

INTRODUCTION

A friend once confided to the poet Alfred Lord Tennyson, 'My dearest hope is to leave the world a better place than I found it.' 'Mine,' responded Tennyson, 'is to have a clearer vision of God.' The latter should be the Christian's supreme calling and where it is pursued the former is realized also. For the person who by God's self-revelation begins to see 'the glory of God in the face of Jesus Christ' and is 'transformed into the same image from glory to glory just as by the Spirit of the Lord' (2 Cor. 3:18; 4:6) will certainly leave the world a better place than he found it.

For most people today, the vision of God is blurred and distorted. Even if they are prepared to recognise His existence they, by ignorance or unbelief, fail to seek the knowledge of God in the only place where it truly can be found – that is, in His revelation of Himself through Holy Scripture, the Bible. The highest study that can ever engage the human mind is surely the being and character of God, the Creator and Ruler of the universe. As we shall see below, it is what we were created for, and because God is infinite it will occupy and enthral us 'world without end.' To disregard the study of God is to impoverish ourselves. It is to go through life blindfolded, as it were, with no sense of direction and no understanding of why we are here and where we are headed.

Consider these often-quoted words of C.H. Spurgeon, in a sermon on Malachi 3:6:

> It has been said by someone that 'the proper study of mankind is man.' I will not oppose the idea, but I believe it is equally true that the proper study of God's elect is God; the proper study of a Christian is the Godhead. The highest science, the loftiest speculation, the mightiest philosophy, which can ever engage the attention of a child of God, is the name, the nature, the person, the work, the doings, and the existence of the great God whom he calls his Father.
>
> There is something exceedingly *improving to the mind* in a contemplation of the Divinity. It is a subject so vast, that all our thoughts are lost in its immensity; so deep, that our pride is drowned in its infinity. Other subjects we can compass and grapple with; in them we feel a kind of self-content, and go our way with the thought, 'Behold, I am wise'. But when we come to this master-science, finding that our plumb-line cannot sound its depth, and that our eagle eye cannot see its height, we turn away with the thought that vain man would be wise, but he is like a wild ass's colt; and with solemn exclamation, 'I am but of yesterday, and know nothing'. No subject of contemplation will tend more to humble the mind, than thoughts of God ...
>
> But while the subject *humbles* the mind, it also *expands* it. He who often thinks of God, will have a larger mind than the man who simply plods around this narrow globe ... The most excellent study for expanding the soul, is the science of Christ, and Him crucified, and the knowledge of the Godhead in the glorious Trinity. Nothing will so enlarge the intellect,

nothing so magnify the whole soul of man, as a devout, earnest, continued investigation of the great subject of the Deity.[1]

It is a very difficult subject, I know, but it is vitally important. So let us begin at the beginning.

THE EXISTENCE OF GOD IS OBVIOUS

The Bible nowhere attempts to prove the existence of God. It simply begins with the words, 'In the beginning God created the heavens and the earth' (Gen. 1:1). The Bible assumes the existence of God. How else could the world have been created, if it was not the work of an intelligent Supreme Being who created it out of nothing? There are those who would say that the creation of the world can be equally well explained as a *chance event*. The problem with that explanation, however, is that you have to believe in a whole series of chance events at incredible odds to account for everything that transpired. To quote John Benton:

> If, for example, we look at our own planet, even at the inorganic level, the fact that although there are many stars in the universe of greatly varying sizes, ages and states of stability, yet we just happen to have a nice, middle-aged, friendly one at the centre of our solar system is by chance. The fact that our planet is at just the right distance from the sun, so as to make it neither too hot nor too cold, is by chance. The fact that our planet's size is such that gravity is neither so great as to crush, nor too little so as not to be able to retain atmosphere, is by chance. Again, the helpful rotational period of the planet is neither too slow, so as to cause impossible temperature variations, nor too fast so as to cause impossible cyclonic conditions; that also is a chance situation. This continual turning to

1. C.H. Spurgeon, *New Park Street Pulpit* (Pilgrim Publications, n.d.), 1855: No. 1, p. 1.

chance just goes on and on and as yet we have not even begun to talk about the chances surrounding the actual origin of life, the so-called 'primeval soup', or the chances involved in the theories of the evolution of all the species by possible mutations in genetic material ... The account of chance is overdrawn at the bank of credibility.[2]

God's creation is a miraculous masterpiece displaying His power and majesty. John Calvin called it a theatre of the glory of God. For those with eyes to see, it is evident that behind the natural order is a mighty and majestic Creator. To deny the existence of God is a sin against knowledge. It is a culpable offence against God as the apostle Paul so plainly states in Romans 1:18-25,

> For the wrath of God is revealed from heaven against all ungodliness and unrighteousness of men, who suppress the truth in unrighteousness, because what may be known of God is manifest in them, for God has shown it to them. For since the creation of the world His invisible attributes are clearly seen, being understood by the things that are made, even His eternal power and Godhead, so that they are without excuse, because, although they knew God, they did not glorify Him as God, nor were thankful, but became futile in their thoughts, and their foolish hearts were darkened. Professing to be wise, they became fools, and changed the glory of the incorruptible God into an image made like corruptible man – and birds and four-footed animals and creeping things. Therefore God also gave them up to uncleanness, in the lusts of their hearts, to dishonor their bodies among themselves, who exchanged the truth of God for the lie [of idolatry], and worshiped and served the creature rather than the Creator, who is blessed forever. Amen.

---

2. John Benton, *Is Christianity True?* (Evangelical Press, 1988), p. 48.

This reliable evidence from the natural order constitutes the content of general revelation, so called because everyone receives it just by virtue of living in the world, beholding and enjoying God's creation. This knowledge of the existence of God has been part of human experience since the beginning of history. In Acts 17:27-28 Paul quotes a Greek poet as witness that human beings acknowledge their divine creation. Talking to the philosophers in Athens, he says, 'He [God] is not far from each of us; for in Him we live and move and have our being, as also some of your own poets have said: "For we are also His offspring."' He also affirms the goodness of the Creator: '...the living God ... in bygone generations allowed all nations to walk in their own ways. Nevertheless He did not leave Himself without witness, in that He did good, gave us rain from heaven and fruitful seasons, filling our hearts with good and gladness' (Acts 14:16-17). Moreover at least some of the demands of His holy law are known to every human conscience, bringing the fear of accountability and eventual retributive judgment (Rom. 2:14-15; 1:32). Failure to thank and serve the Creator in righteousness is sin against the universal revelation of His almighty power, supreme praiseworthiness, and moral claim on all human beings. Most people, looking at our universe, see the hand of design, not the blind stumbling of chance. The case for the existence of God is very plain. It does not need to be proved to an open and honest mind. All human beings have a deep inner sense that God exists, 'because what may be known of God is manifest to them, for God has shown it to them' (Rom. 1:19). It is something that remains in all of us, because we are created in the image of God. Sin cannot get rid of it. That is Paul's sweeping claim.

THE LIVING GOD IS A SELF-REVEALING GOD

To love and serve the Creator in righteousness, men and women need something more than an awareness of His existence through general revelation. Humankind also needs to know who and what He is, where He can be found, and how He may be approached. This knowledge only God Himself can reveal to us, and so He supplemented general revelation with the further revelation of Himself as the God and Saviour of sinners through Jesus Christ. This revelation, given over many centuries and recorded in the Bible, is called special revelation because it was specifically given to some for the benefit of all. Through it God revealed the nature of His being, character and will to 'holy men of God' whom He called His prophets, and what He revealed to them, they in turn recorded in the Bible for all humanity. All the books of the Bible owe their origin to God. 'For', says the apostle Peter, 'prophecy never came by the will of man, but holy men of God spoke as they were moved by the Holy Spirit' (2 Pet. 1:21). Paul says, 'All Scripture is given by inspiration of God' [literally, 'is God-breathed', 2 Tim. 3:16]. So the words they wrote were the very words God intended to be the means of revealing His glorious attributes and gracious purposes. As a result, we do not have to guess what God is like. God, through the prophets of the Old Testament and the apostles of the New, has told us all we need to know about Himself in order to worship and serve Him aright. But why was His self-revelation necessary? The Bible gives us two answers.

Because God is invisible

The Bible tells us that God is a Spirit (John 4:24). He does not have a body, as we do. He is invisible. The apostle Paul says that He is a God 'whom no man has seen or can see' (1 Tim. 6:16), so He cannot be known or measured by our physical senses. It is true that we sometimes read in the Bible of His eyes, His ears, His mouth, and so on, but these are just human figures of speech, or anthropomorphisms. They cannot be taken literally, because God has no body. They are simply a way of telling us that God sees and hears everything, and that God can communicate with us. When the Bible says that some people saw God, it means that they saw the glory of God, but not God Himself; just as we do not see the sun itself, but the sunshine. Only in heaven shall we see God, because only then shall we be given new spiritual faculties which will enable us to see Him like the angels do. Meanwhile, God remains invisible to us. However, we must not think of Him as simply an invisible force like the wind or electricity or magnetism. God is a personal Spirit. He is not a something, but *Someone.* He is not a supreme power (deism), but a Supreme Being (theism) whom the Bible says has all the attributes of personality. God thinks, God communicates, God loves, God has a will and acts upon it. Psalm 94:9-10 says, 'He who planted the ear, shall He not hear? He who formed the eye, shall He not see? He who instructs the nations, shall He not correct?'

Indeed, God is not only personal but goes beyond our ordinary concept of personality. There is a super-abundance of personality in God, for He is tri-personal. He exists in the mystery of the Trinity: one God in three persons (Father, Son and Holy Spirit) who are not three gods, but one God. These are facts about God that we could never have known, unless God in His goodness chose to reveal them to us through His prophets and apostles.

Secondly, it was necessary for God to reveal Himself to mankind –

Because God is infinite

Finite man cannot possibly comprehend the nature of the being and character of God, the Creator, who is infinite. The idea of such a task moves us to identify with the words of Zophar in Job 11:7-9, 'Can you search out the deep things of God? Can you find out the limits of the Almighty? They are higher than heaven – what can you do? Deeper than Sheol – what can you know? Their measure is longer than the earth, and broader than the sea.' Truly, when we try, for example, to fathom God's eternity, His omnipresence, His omniscience, His omnipotence, our minds are overwhelmed. But as A.W. Pink cautions: 'The incomprehensibility of the Divine nature is not a reason why we should desist from reverent inquiry and prayerful strivings to apprehend what He has so graciously revealed of Himself in His word.'[3]

Now in the Bible the infinity of God is usually contrasted with the finiteness of man. Man is confined and limited, but God is infinite, unlimited, boundless, immeasurable in every part of His being. For example, when we think of God and space, He is *everywhere*. Jeremiah 23:24 says, '"Can anyone hide himself in secret places, so I shall not see him?" says the LORD. "Do I not fill heaven and earth?" says the LORD.' What an amazing truth! Most people think that God is stationed in heaven; but God is an infinite Spirit and the totality of His being fills all places at all times. There is, of course, a particular manifestation of His presence in heaven on His throne; but His essence is as much on earth as it is in heaven. Augustine, the bishop of Hippo in the fifth century, said, 'God is a circle whose centre is everywhere and whose circumference is nowhere.' It is a difficult concept. Our finite minds cannot take

---

3. A.W. Pink, *The Attributes of God* (Baker Book House, 2004), p. 88.

it in. All we can do is believe what God has declared concerning Himself and bow in worship and wonder.

In relation to time, God is *eternal*. There are three types of existence according to Scripture. There is *life that begins and then ends*, which is the life of plants and animals. Then there is *life that begins but has no end*. This is the life God has given to angels and men. Men and angels will spend eternity either in bliss or in misery. And then, again, there is *life that has neither beginning nor ending*. Such is the amazing duration of God's existence. Moses says, 'Before the mountains were brought forth, or ever You had formed the earth and the world, even from everlasting to everlasting, You are God' (Ps. 90:2). Everything owes its beginning to God, but He Himself has no beginning. He is the God who is, who always has been, and always will be. All things depend on Him for their existence, but His own existence does not depend on anything or anyone other than Himself.

When it comes to knowledge, God *knows everything*. Psalm 147:5 says, 'Great is our Lord ... His understanding is infinite.' As humans, we learn by degrees. We increase in knowledge, but our knowledge is always limited. For God, however, there is no such thing as learning or gaining knowledge. He has always known all things as they really are. There is nothing of which He is ignorant or uncertain, and that means He cannot be surprised or deceived.

Again, in the realm of power, God is *almighty*. Psalm 115:3 says, 'Our God is in heaven; He does whatever He pleases.' He has unlimited power which, guided by His infinite wisdom, always does what is right; and guided by His infinite purity, always does what is good. So although what God says about Himself is clear enough, it is all too wonderful for our finite minds to comprehend. We cannot take it in, because God's thoughts and God's ways are higher than ours (Isa. 55:8-9). We can see the truth of all the above, but we cannot explain *how* it can be so. Only God can fathom God (1 Cor. 2:11). Can anyone explain how it is possible for God to exist as a personal being, without a body? Or how He can see without eyes, or hear without ears, or speak without a mouth? Can anyone grasp how all of God can be in all places at all times? Or how He can be without beginning and without end? Our puny minds are baffled when we try to think of what it means to be all-knowing, or how God can be the author of all things and not be the author of sin? Truly, no question about God that contains the word *how* can be answered. Our finite minds are too poor for that.

Questions, however, that contain the word *what* can be answered plainly and clearly, because God has revealed the answers in the Bible. We are able to study what God has said in His word, and we are able to know what the truth is, but we are not able to explain how it can be so. We are overwhelmed by what we learn. The more we consider it, the more we realise that there is no appropriate reaction to what we have learned other than to fall down and adore Him, our great and awesome Creator. We rejoice that God in His goodness has revealed so much about Himself in Scripture, and we trust His perfect wisdom in choosing to reveal no more. For as mere creatures we would never have known what the invisible and infinite God was like, but what He has revealed is surely more than enough to make us true worshippers of Him. This is what Moses is saying in Deuteronomy 29:29, 'The secret things belong to the LORD our God, but those things which are revealed belong to us and our children forever, that we may do all the words of this law.'

For those who are seeking to correctly evaluate the evidence at hand, everything in nature and everything in Scripture proves clearly that God exists and that He is the almighty and all-wise Creator that Scripture describes Him to be. 'Therefore,' says Wayne Grudem, 'when we believe that God exists, we are basing our belief *not* on some blind hope apart from any evidence, but on *an overwhelming amount of reliable evidence from God's word and God's works*. It is a characteristic of true faith that it is a confidence based on reliable evidence, and faith in the existence of God shares this characteristic. Furthermore, these evidences can all be seen as valid proofs for the existence of God, even though some people reject them. This does not mean that the evidence is invalid in itself, only that those who reject the evidence are evaluating it wrongly.'[4]

WHAT IS AN ATTRIBUTE?

An attribute is a quality belonging naturally (intrinsically) to someone or something. It is not the essence of what is being referred to, but a quality characteristic of it. To quote A.W. Tozer, a great American preacher of the twentieth century,

> An attribute of God is not that of which God is composed. The very fact that God is God indicates that God isn't 'composed' at all ... Anything that is composed has to have been composed by someone, and the composer is greater than the composition ... But God is not made! Therefore, we cannot say that the attributes are the part of which God is made, because God is not made of parts ... God's attributes are not God ... I say that God is holy, but holiness is not God. I say that God is wisdom, but wisdom is not God. God is God! The Christian believes that God is the original

4. Wayne Grudem, *Systematic Theology*, (Zondervan, 1994), p. 143.

existence, that He said 'I AM.' And because God is, everything else that is, is.[5]

What, then, are some of the attributes of God? We cannot find a more simple answer than that given in *The Westminster Shorter Catechism for Children* under the fourth question: 'What is God?' The answer given is short, but sufficient: 'God is a Spirit, infinite, eternal, and unchangeable in His being, wisdom, power, holiness, justice, goodness and truth.' The attributes of God are the qualities belonging to, or characteristic of Deity, which set Him apart from all of creation and mark the difference and distance between the Creator and His creatures. They are natural and moral qualities relating to His being (or essence) and character. The natural qualities manifest the greatness of God's being, such as His eternity, His omnipotence, His omnipresence, His omniscience, and so on. The moral qualities manifest the goodness of God's character, such as His holiness, His love, His faithfulness, and His justice, to name a few.

CLASSIFYING GOD'S ATTRIBUTES

In studying the attributes of God, it is important to distinguish between those that belong to His being or essence and those that belong to His character. The former are termed his *incommunicable attributes* and the latter His *communicable attributes*. The attributes of God's being are incommunicable because He does not and cannot share or communicate any of them with any other being, human or angelic. They are the unique property of deity. Deity cannot be shared or passed on to other beings because deity is eternal. It has no beginning or end. Thus the first eight chapters of this book deal with the incommunicable attributes of God's being (His

---

5. A.W. Tozer, *The Attributes of God*, (Christian Publications, 2001), vol. 2, pp. 16-17.

transcendence, triunity, omnipresence, omniscience, wisdom, omnipotence, providence and immutability).

The last seven chapters deal with the communicable attributes of God's character which in His gracious goodness He has and He does share with humankind (His holiness, love, grace, faithfulness, jealousy, wrath and glory). They are communicable, because when God created man, He communicated to him finite qualities corresponding to His own infinite moral attributes. This is what Scripture means when it says that 'God created man in His own image' (Gen. 1:27). God created man a free spiritual being with a nature that was good, holy, loving, truthful and godly, so that he could commune with his Creator and respond to Him. These moral qualities given by God to man, however, were lost at the Fall, from which time the image of God was universally marred in humankind. All men and women are now ungodly by nature (cf. Eccles. 7:29). But God never gives up on His eternal purposes. From the Fall, in fulfilment of His eternal plan of redemption, God has been unceasingly at work in the lives of His believing people to repair His ruined image by communicating these godly moral qualities to them afresh (2 Cor. 3:18; Col. 3:10). Only at the resurrection will the image of God be fully restored in His saints, and only in the new heaven and the new earth will redeemed and glorified men and women know as much of the divine character as it is possible for a perfect finite human being to know. So in the end we need to realise that however helpful this distinction may be, there is no divine attribute that is *completely* communicable, because God is infinitely perfect and we can never become as infinitely perfect as God is.

THE INESTIMABLE BLESSING OF KNOWING GOD PERSONALLY

It is our greatest privilege

We pride ourselves if we know great and important people, but who is greater and more important than Almighty God? Moreover, this is precisely what God created the angels and human beings for. It was not because He needed their company or their worship. Before creation the three persons of the Godhead were completely fulfilled in each other's company, attention and love. 'In the beginning God' (Gen. 1:1). There was no need of anyone or anything else. None! God's creation of men and angels added nothing to His eternal and perfect fullness. His divine glory cannot be increased or decreased. Rather, the creation of men and angels was an act of sovereign grace in which He generously provided them with the unequalled privilege of beholding with rapture the glory of His divine infinite perfections. God's communion with Adam and Eve in the Garden of Eden at creation was just a foretaste of what was to come for the human race if it continued in sinless fellowship with Him.

Indeed, when the divine plan for creation is finally accomplished by redemption through Christ, Scripture says: 'the earth shall be full of the knowledge of the LORD as the waters cover the sea' (Isa. 11:9); and again, 'No more shall every man teach his neighbour, and every man his brother, saying, "Know the LORD," for they all shall know Me, from the least of them to the greatest of them, says the LORD' (Jer. 31:34). Until then we are to continually 'grow in the grace and knowledge of our Lord and Saviour Jesus Christ' (2 Pet. 3:18).

Our ultimate aim, then, in studying what God has revealed about Himself in the Bible must be to know God personally; to be enraptured with His glory and love Him forever. God has given us the Bible, not just to fill our heads with lofty and amazing concepts of Himself. The pursuit of theological knowledge for its own sake will only make us proud and conceited. We will tend to look down on those less informed. For as Paul warned the conceited Corinthians, 'Knowledge puffs up, but love [for God] edifies. And if anyone thinks that he knows anything, he knows nothing yet as he ought to know. But if anyone loves God, this one is known by Him' (1 Cor. 8:1-3). That must be the goal of all our study of God. God in His Word insists on it. He does not want to be just the object of our study, but the object of our love: '"You shall love the LORD your God with all your heart, with all your soul, and with all your mind." This is the first and great commandment' (Matt. 22:37-38). It is to be our supreme passion, honour and delight, because God is worthy of no less. 'Thus says the LORD: "Let not the wise man glory in his wisdom, let not the mighty man glory in his might, nor let the rich man glory in his riches; but let him who glories glory in this, that he understands and knows Me, that I am the LORD, exercising lovingkindness, judgment, and righteousness in the earth. For in these I delight" says the LORD' (Jer. 9:23-24; cf. Hosea 6:3; Phil. 3:8).

It is our greatest need

Thus our Lord Jesus Christ's prayer for us in John 17:3 is, 'This is eternal life, that they may know You, the only true God, and Jesus Christ whom You have sent.' All who are rightly related to God and His Son, the fountain of life, enjoy eternal life (2 Tim. 1:10). The only reason why human beings die is that sin has cut us off from God. Isaiah 59:2 says, 'Your iniquities have separated you from your God.' Sin cuts us off from the divine Source of life. The Bible therefore says, 'The soul who sins shall die' (Ezek. 18:20); and again, 'The wages of sin is death' (Rom. 6:23). That is why God sent His only begotten Son to the world. He came to pay the penalty of our sin by dying in our place on the cross. He came to remove sin's offence. Thus Peter says, 'Christ also suffered once for sins, the just for the unjust, that He might bring us to God' (1 Pet. 3:18). Paul states it more fully in 2 Corinthians 5:19-21, 'God was in Christ reconciling the world to Himself, not imputing their trespasses to them ... For He [God] made Him [Christ] who knew no sin to be sin for us, that we might become the righteousness of God in Him.' Our Lord Jesus said, 'He who believes in the Son has everlasting life; and he who does not believe the Son shall not see life, but the wrath of God abides on him' (John 3:36).

What the Bible is clearly saying is that if we come to Christ in faith, we can be justly pardoned and reconciled to God, the Source of eternal life. Eternal life is not just life that has no end. Life in hell will have no end! Eternal life is to know God and live in the joy and favour of His presence forever. Of course, the fullness of that eternal life and felicity will only be enjoyed in heaven because sin will be no more; 'God will wipe away every tear from their eyes; there shall be no more death, nor sorrow, nor crying. There shall be no more pain, for the former things have passed away' (Rev. 21:4). But even here on earth we can begin to enjoy eternal life in ever-increasing measure as we come to know God more and more through His Son, Jesus Christ (John 5:24). Thus Paul's prayer for every believer in Christ is: 'that you may walk worthy of the Lord, fully pleasing Him, being fruitful in every good work and increasing in the knowledge of God' (Col. 1:10).

What an inestimable blessing it is to know God! Do not discount it. Heed the words of Job 22:21-22, 'Now acquaint yourself with Him, and be at peace; thereby good will come to you. Receive, please, instruction from His mouth, and lay up His words in your heart.' What instruction has God given us? These are His words: 'Believe in the Lord Jesus Christ, and you will be saved' (Acts 16:31); and again, 'Nor is there salvation in any other, for there is no other name under heaven given among men by which we must be saved' (Acts 4:12). Jesus is 'able to save to the uttermost those who come to God through Him, since He always lives to make intercession for them' (Heb. 7:25). If we have not yet done so, let us believe in Jesus Christ as our Saviour now, for He will respond immediately to our faith; 'the one who comes to Me I will by no means cast out' (John 6:37).

If we are Christians, let us take these words upon our hearts and lips:

Day by day, dear Lord,
Of Thee three things I pray:
To see Thee more clearly
To love Thee more dearly
To follow Thee more nearly.

(Prayer of Richard of Chichester, 1197-1253)

PART I:

THE INCOMMUNICABLE ATTRIBUTES OF GOD'S BEING

PART I.

1

THE TRANSCENDENCE OF GOD

Can you search out the deep things of God?
Can you find out the limits of the Almighty?
They are higher than heaven – what can you do?
Deeper than Sheol – what can you know? (Job 11:7-8).

Great is the LORD, and greatly to be praised;
And His greatness is unsearchable (Ps. 145:3).

'For My thoughts are not your thoughts,
Nor are your ways My ways,' says the LORD.
'For as the heavens are higher than the earth,
So are My ways higher than your ways,
And My thoughts than your thoughts' (Isa. 55:8-9).

The term *transcendence* when used with reference to
God simply means that He exists apart from and not
subject to the limitations of the created order. The Bible
teaches that God is distinct from His creation. He is
not part of it, for He created it and sustains it. By His
omnipresence God fills the whole of creation with the
whole of His being, but He is in no way confined to
it. Rather God transcends all of creation, because He

is much greater than creation and He is independent of it. This is true not only of God's omnipresence (His presence everywhere all the time) and His omnipotence (His almighty power), but of all the attributes of God's being and God's character.

Novatian of Rome, a theologian of the third century, vividly put it like this:

> The mind of man cannot fittingly conceive how great is God and how majestic His nature ... Whatever can be thought about Him is less than He; whatever can be uttered about Him will be less than He when compared with Him. When we are silent, we can experience Him to some extent, but we cannot express Him in words as He really is. If the keen sight of our eyes grows dim by looking at the sun so that their gaze is overpowered by the bright rays that meet them, so our mental vision undergoes this very thing in its every thought of God. The more it endeavours to contemplate God, the more it is blinded by the light of its own thought. What can you say about Him that is worthy of Him – He who is more sublime than all sublimity, loftier than all loftiness, more profound than all profundity, brighter than all light, more brilliant than all brilliance, more splendid than all splendour, mightier than all might, more powerful than all power, more beautiful than all beauty, truer than all truth, stronger than all strength, greater than all majesty, more potent than all potency, richer than all riches, kinder than all kindness, better than all goodness, more just than all justice, and more merciful than all mercy? Every kind of virtue must of necessity be less than He who is the God and Author of them all. Nothing really can be compared to Him, for He is above everything that can be said of Him.[1]

---

1. Adapted from Novatian in *Ante-Nicene Christian Library*, vol. xxiii (T & T Clark, 1869). Quoted by Steve Halliday and William Travis, *How Great Thou Art* (Multinomah Publishers, 1999), January 2.

Supremely the transcendence of God is seen in His tripersonality. Right at the beginning of the Bible in the story of creation a plurality of persons is at work. Thus we read, 'In the beginning God created the heavens and the earth ... Then God said, "Let *us* make man in *our* image according to *our* likeness"' (Gen. 1:1,26, italics added). The Speaker and Creator in verse 26 is the same Person Paul refers to in Ephesians 4:6 as 'one God and Father of all, who is above all, and through all, and in you all.' But although God the Father was the primary agent in initiating the act of creation, Scripture reveals that God the Son and God the Holy Spirit were also active in creation. Of the Son it is said, 'In the beginning was the Word, and the Word was with God, and the Word was God. He was in the beginning with God. All things were made through Him, and without Him nothing was made that was made ... And the Word became flesh and dwelt among us' (John 1:1-3,14; see also Col. 1:16; Heb. 1:2). Regarding the Holy Spirit, Genesis 1:2 says that at creation 'the Spirit of God was hovering over the face of the waters' (cf. Job 33:4; Ps. 104:30). In eternity past, from everlasting, there was only one God in three Persons (Father, Son, Holy Spirit) coequal, coeternal, and of the same essence, distinct but not separate. Accordingly, G.E. Lane writes, 'God is so infinitely great that He cannot adequately be expressed in one person. So manifold are His attributes and so numerous His activities that Three persons are required to do justice to them! Not that God divides Himself between the Three. Each one contains the fullness of the Godhead severally, and yet together, make up but One God.'[2] The triunity of God is the chief doctrine which does justice to the transcendence of God's being.

---

2. G.E. Lane, *Foundations of the Faith* (Sovereign Grace Union, n.d.), No. 2, p. 9.

GOD IS BOTH TRANSCENDENT AND IMMANENT
IN CREATION

Although God is much greater than all creation and independent of it, He is also very much involved in it, for it is perpetually dependent on Him for its existence and maintenance. Thus in His relationship to His creation God is described as being not only *transcendent* but also *immanent* (remaining in it). The God of the Bible is not a God who is detached from creation. Rather He is a God who through Christ is continually 'upholding all things by the word of His power' (Heb. 1:3); who 'gives to all life, breath, and all things,' and 'in Him we live and move and have our being' (Acts 17:25,28).

Now because God is both transcendent and immanent in His relationship with His creation, there are two heretical viewpoints we must refute. The first error is *pantheism* which views all of creation as God. God therefore has no personality. His essence is material. Again, the God of pantheism is not unchanging, because as creation changes, so He must change. And yet again, God cannot be holy, because the evil that is in the world must also be a part of God. The goal of pantheism is the absorption of individual human personality into creation as raindrops are swallowed up in the ocean. The other error is *deism* which views God as transcendent but not immanent in creation. The Creator is likened to a divine clockmaker who in the beginning wound up everything and then left it to run on its own. It dismisses the Bible's history of God's involvement in nature and human affairs. So any activity like praying to God or worshipping God is senseless because God is removed and uninvolved in creation. How great is our debt of gratitude to God for the revelation in Scripture of both His transcendence and His immanence in creation.

Heaven and earth cannot contain Him (1 Kings 8:27; Isa. 66:1; Acts 7:48,49), and at the same time He fills both and 'is not far from each one of us' (Ps. 139:7-10; Jer. 23:23,24; Acts 17:27,28).

THE INFINITY, ETERNITY AND HOLINESS OF GOD

Nowhere in Scripture is the transcendence of God more beautifully stated than in Isaiah 57:15, 'For thus says the High and Lofty One who inhabits eternity, whose name is Holy: "I dwell in the high and holy place, with him who has a contrite and humble spirit, to revive the spirit of the humble, and to revive the heart of the contrite ones."' The situation underlying Isaiah 57 is strikingly similar to our own. It was an age that had forgotten God and no longer gave Him a thought (v. 11). So in verse 15 God distinguishes Himself from those whom He says 'have not remembered Me, nor taken it to your heart ... that you do not fear Me.' And He says in effect: You cannot dismiss Me like that; I am not a figment of human imagination. I am above all created existence. I am self-existent, 'the High and Lofty One'. That means that God is not bound by *space*. He infinitely transcends any of our human measurements. He is beyond man's reach and far above his thoughts. He is our Creator, and we are His creatures. We are confined and limited, but He is infinite, unlimited and boundless.

Nor is God bound by *time*. He says, 'I am the One who inhabits eternity.' We are confined to clocks and calendars. We have a beginning and an end; God does not. God has always existed; He continues to exist and He will always exist. All things depend on God, but He does not depend on anything or anyone for His existence. Of course, when God created us He also necessarily created time. So we have to think in terms of a succession of time. Thus, for instance, we speak of God doing things in the past and our hope of His doing things in the future. But although it is correct to speak like that, we have to understand that God is above time and does not change with time. He lives in eternity. As the Eternal One, God is completely free from the world of time in which we live. *Before* and *after* do not have the same restrictive significance for Him as they do for us. We are the slaves of time, God is its Master. Time has an effect on us, but it has no effect on God. He is unchangeably the same: 'Of old You laid the foundation of the earth, and the heavens are the work of Your hands. They will perish, but You will endure; yes, they will all grow old like a garment; like a cloak You will change them, and they will be changed. But You are the same, and Your years will have no end' (Ps. 102:25-27; Heb. 13:8).

There is a precious verse in James 1:17 which says that God is 'the Father of lights, with whom there is no variation or shadow of turning.' In other words, God created the sun and the moon to divide day and night, and create variation and change in our world. We see shadows lengthening on the earth in a physical way as the sun rises and sets. That is part of the world in which we live. But the Scripture says that God is the 'Father of lights' who is in control of all these things, and so with Him 'there is no variation or shadow due to change' (ESV). The sun does not rise and set on the Creator. There are no changes in time or space that affect God. He is above and beyond this created world and everything that happens in it.

This is a vision of God we all desperately need if we are to have any hope in this world or the next. Indeed, it was this vision that strengthened and fortified Isaiah himself. He lived and served God in the seventh century BC when things in Judah could not have been gloomier. But in chapter 6:1 the prophet says, 'In the year that King Uzziah died, I saw the LORD sitting on a throne, high and lifted up.' Isaiah lived during the reign of four kings, Uzziah being the first and most successful of them. So when Uzziah died (c. 739 B.C.), things looked really bleak for the nation. But then the prophet had this vision of God ruling from a throne, high and lifted up above all other thrones, with unrivalled and unchallenged majesty.

Isaiah, however, saw something else that is also emphasised in chapter 57; namely, that the name of the High and Lofty One who inhabits eternity is 'holy'. So the prophet tells us in chapter 6:3 of the seraphim around God's throne, and 'one cried to another and said: Holy, holy, holy is the LORD of hosts.' Holiness is God's moral transcendence over persons rather than things. It is His separateness from all other beings, both men and angels. He is the *one apart*. He is absolute purity; unsullied even by the shadow of sin in the universe. For the Bible says, 'God is light; and in Him is no darkness at all' (1 John 1:5). The Greek word for 'holy' refers to an object full of awesome purity. Paul therefore speaks of God 'dwelling in unapproachable light, whom no man has seen or can see' (1 Tim. 6:16). He is the wholly other, who stands in utter contrast to all other beings, even holy angels who can still sin. Thus the seraphim covered their faces with their wings (v. 2), because the holiness of God was too bright and glorious to gaze on. Little wonder, then, that Isaiah as a sinful, fallen creature, could not restrain himself from crying out: 'Woe is me, for I am undone! Because I am a man of unclean lips, and I dwell in the midst of a people of unclean lips. For my eyes have seen the King, the LORD of hosts' (v. 5).

Every human encounter with God in the Bible has a similar response. Abraham, after pleading for Sodom to be spared destruction, says, 'I who am but dust and ashes have taken it upon myself to speak to the LORD' (Gen. 18:27). Job says to God, 'I have heard of You by the hearing of the ear, but now my eye sees You. Therefore I abhor myself and repent in dust and ashes' (Job 42:6). Peter, when he realised the holiness and divinity of Jesus Christ, said, 'Depart from me; for I am a sinful man, O Lord' (Luke 5:8).

Do we stand in awe of God, 'the High and Lofty One who inhabits eternity, whose name is Holy'? When Isaiah went to the temple and had a vision of God, there was not the flippancy that we see in many churches today where preachers seek to entertain their congregations with human wit and senseless personal anecdotes. Tozer spoke out about it near the end of his life (1963): 'I'm concerned about our flippancy these days. It is a terrible sin in the presence of a holy God. What if you and your friends were in the presence of the Queen of England and someone started trying to be funny by telling jokes about queens? How shameful, how horrible it would be! No one would do such a thing. And yet, she's only a woman, a human being like you. How much more terrible that we can be so flippant in the presence of the great God, who is Lord of all lords and King of all kings!'[3]

The situation has only become worse in our day. Here are some messages that I have seen displayed on notice boards outside churches in the area where I live: 'God is like Coke – He's the real thing!' 'God is like Bayer Aspirin – He works wonders!' 'God is like your American Express card – don't leave home without Him!' It is blasphemy being 'witty' about

___
3. A.W. Tozer, *The Attributes of God vol. 2*, pp. 45-46.

God or the things of God. Nor is it honouring to hear preachers calling upon people to 'Give God a chance.' Or applauding preachers, testimonies, singers and baptismal candidates for serving God.

As Pink explains:

> It is perfectly true that God is both honoured and dishonoured by men; not in His essential being, but in His official character. It is equally true that God has been 'glorified' by creation, by providence, and by redemption. This we do not and dare not dispute for a moment. But all of this has to do with His manifestative glory and the recognition of it by us. Yet had God so pleased He might have continued alone for all eternity, *without making known* His glory unto creatures. Whether He should do so or not was determined solely by His own will. He was perfectly blessed in Himself before the first creature was called into being. And what are all the creatures of His hands *unto Him* even now? Let Scripture again make answer: 'Behold, the nations are as a drop of a bucket, and are counted as the small dust of the balance ... All nations before Him are as *nothing*; and they are counted to Him less than nothing, and vanity. To whom then will ye liken God? Or what likeness will ye compare unto Him? ... It is He that sitteth upon the circle of the earth, and the inhabitants thereof are as grasshoppers; that stretcheth out the heavens as a curtain, and spreadeth them out as a tent to dwell in: that bringeth the princes to nothing; He maketh the judges of the earth as vanity' (Isa. 40:15-23). How vastly different is the God of Scripture from the 'god' of the average pulpit![4]

Many of our modern religious songs have not helped either to stem the flood of low and unworthy views of God in our churches. With popular little ditties that have no real theology and much mindless repetition,

---

4. A.W. Pink, *The Attributes of God*, p. 11.

nobody is likely to leave our places of worship smitten low by the sheer, unsullied majesty of 'the High and Lofty One who inhabits eternity, whose name is Holy.' Many are deeply troubled by the modern trend to focus on our spiritual experience and dismiss the great theological hymns of the past three centuries by people like Isaac Watts, Charles Wesley, John Newton and Fanny Crosby (to name only a few), which focus on the greatness of God's being and the perfection of His character. Why ignore words like, 'Before Jehovah's aweful throne, ye nations bow with sacred joy. Know that the Lord is God alone; He can create, and He destroy'? Or, 'And can it be that I should gain an interest in the Saviour's blood? Died He for me, who caused His pain? For me, who Him to death pursued? Amazing love! How can it be that Thou, my God, should'st die for me?'

What is the difference between great hymns like these and many of our modern spiritual songs? Some would say that the difference is that the old hymns are out-of-date; whereas the new songs are contemporary and 'with-it'. But that is not the real difference, is it? The real difference is that the old hymns have a view of God that is biblical and inspire awe and wonder. Contemporary songs, on the other hand, often have a low and sentimental view of God that do little to convey His transcendence to those who sing them. The message of our text is that there is an infinite gulf fixed between the great I AM and all created things. God is of an essence to the likes of which nothing in the universe can be compared. He is above all, and the little we do know of God is only what in His grace He has been pleased to make known through His Holy Word. It is, however, enough to make us fall down in reverent fear and awesome wonder and confess with the hymnwriter:

Eternal Light! Eternal Light!
How pure the soul must be,
When, placed within Thy searching sight,
It shrinks not, but with calm delight
Can live, and look on Thee.

The spirits that surround Thy throne
May bear the burning bliss,
But that is surely theirs alone,
Since they have never, never known
A fallen world like this.

O how shall I, whose native sphere
Is dark, whose mind is dim,
Before the ineffable appear,
And on my naked spirit bear
The uncreated beam?

There is a way for man to rise
To that sublime abode –
An offering and a sacrifice,
A Holy Spirit's energies,
An advocate with God.

These, these prepare us for the sight
Of Holiness above;
The sons of ignorance and night
Can dwell in the eternal light,
Through the eternal love.

(Thomas Binney, 1798-1874)

However, there is something else said in Isaiah 57, and it is totally unexpected.

THE HIGH AND LOFTY ONE DEIGNS TO DWELL WITH EARTH'S LOWLY ONES

In a surprising act of condescension, God says, 'I dwell in the high and holy place' (which is what we would expect, given what we have already learned about God); but then follows the astonishingly gracious disclosure: 'with him who has a contrite and humble spirit, to revive the spirit of the humble, and to revive the heart of the contrite ones.' Here we have the incredible paradox of God's *greatness* and *graciousness.* It was the study of this verse that led one of the old Puritans to say: 'God has two thrones, one in the highest heaven and the other in the lowliest heart!' The problem, however, is that no human being is by nature humble and contrite. We are proud and self-seeking. That is what led to the fall of the human race. Adam and Eve were tempted to think that they could become as great as God, and so they disobeyed God and ate the fruit they thought would make them like God.

From that day to this a usurper (a puppet king called *self*) sits on the throne of every person's heart in the place of God. It is only because of God's unsolicited grace and mercy that He has taken the initiative to win back that place that belongs to Him in the citadel of man's soul. In the consuming fire of His righteous anger and justice, God could just have destroyed the entire human race, but He did not. Instead, 'according to His mercy He saved us' (Titus 3:5), and He did so by humbling our pride and making us contrite. The word 'contrite' literally means to be 'crushed or broken'. It is an exceptionally strong word used of grinding a stone to powder. This is how God must deal with our pride before He can take up His abode within us. Only when we lie as the dust beneath His feet, are we ready for His habitation.

Now God has many ways to accomplish this, some more severe than others, depending on how proud and hard-hearted we are. God can use *affliction* to humble us, and affliction can come in many forms. It can come in the form of drug or alcohol addiction. It can come in the form of divorce, or bankruptcy, or a stroke, or cancer, or bereavement. The High and Lofty One knows what will best humble us, but such drastic means are only resorted to when we have persistently turned a deaf ear to His preferred means of humbling us, which is conviction of sin (of our defiance of His will and disrespect of His Person).

We can never be truly humbled before God as long as we see our sin solely as an injury to ourselves. True, adversity and trouble may lead us to seek God's help, but all too often, as soon as our marriage is repaired, or our financial difficulties solved, or our bodies healed, we go back to thumbing our noses at God. To be truly saved we must see our sin as spiritual high treason and defiance of the Supreme Being of the universe, who is infinitely above and beyond us in the greatness of His being and the perfection of His character. Only such a conviction of sin will bring us to our knees, and only God by His Spirit and through His Word can bring us to such a conviction of sin.

'Proud man', said Augustine, 'would perish unless a lowly God found him.' Indeed, in the person of His Son, Jesus Christ, He stooped so low that He became man and lived among us. He was conceived in the womb of a peasant virgin and born in a stable among the animals: the transcendent God 'contracted to a span; incomprehensibly made man' (Charles Wesley). Why did He do that? He did it because He loved us, and He loved us because 'God is love' (1 John 4:8,16). It was not to gain anything from us; for even at our best we are unlovable. Rather, He did it because we were doomed to eternal destruction without His intervention. Herein lies the incredible mystery of the God of the Bible. The transcendentally awesome

One is also the tenderly affectionate One; the Majestic Sovereign is also the Merciful Saviour. The God who is infinitely above and beyond us came to our planet two thousand years ago and took our flesh in order that He might take away our sin and live in our hearts.

Thus when John the Baptist, the forerunner of Jesus the Christ, first set eyes on Him, he said, 'Behold! The Lamb of God who takes away the sin of the world' (John 1:29). Jesus, who was both God and man in one Person forever, became God's sacrificial Lamb whose blood was shed in an atoning death on the cross for the forgiveness of our sins (Matt. 26:27-28). John the apostle puts it so tenderly in his first epistle when He says, 'In this the love of God was manifested towards us, that God sent His only begotten Son into the world that we might live through Him. In this is love, not that we loved God, but that He loved us and sent His Son to be the propitiation for our sins' (1 John 4:9-10).

Though He is above and beyond us sinful, mortal creatures, God, in an unfathomable mystery, has drawn near to us 'to revive the spirit of the humble.' He says, 'I will not contend forever, nor will I always be angry; for the spirit would fail before Me, and the souls which I have made' (Isa. 57:16). The purpose of divine affliction is to get our attention, so that He can humble our haughty souls, making us contrite for our sins, and then healing our wayward hearts. 'I have seen his ways, and will heal him', says God; 'I will also lead him and restore comfort to him, creating praise on the lips of the mourners in Israel. Peace, peace, to those who are far and near, says the LORD. And I will heal them' (vv.18-19, NIV).

That is the blessing that the Transcendent God and Saviour of the world (John 4:42) bestows on those who mourn over their sins (Matt. 5:4). 'The wicked', on the other hand, 'are like the tossing sea, which cannot rest, whose waves cast up mire and the mud. There is no peace, says my God, for the wicked' (v. 20). Why would anyone continue to resist the humbling of the High and Lofty One, in order to hold on to a troubled life that only washes up muck and dirty foam? To quote J. Gresham Machen (1881-1937), the great spokesman for orthodox biblical Christianity in America:

The Lord who is our shepherd is also the dreadful ruler of all nature whose counsel none can tell. But the curtain has been drawn gently aside. But to whom has a look been granted beyond? Here is the wonder of our religion; here is the strange condescension of God. Not only to the wise and the mighty has a look been granted ... but to plain people whom wise men despise. It is not man's way but God's way. 'I thank thee, O Father,' the Saviour said, 'Lord of heaven and earth, because thou hast hid these things from the wise and prudent, and hast revealed them unto babes. Even so Father: for so it seemed good in thy sight.'

2

THE TRIUNITY OF GOD

The doctrine of the Trinity is the most profound truth to be revealed in God's word, the Bible. No truth of Scripture is as difficult to comprehend as the notion of the triunity of God. It has been accurately defined, but to explain what has been defined in a logical and coherent way is impossible for finite, fallen human minds. The Westminster Larger Catechism gives this definition of the Trinity: 'There are three persons in the Godhead, the Father, the Son, and the Holy Spirit. And these three are one true, eternal God, the same in substance, equal in power and glory, although distinguished by their personal properties (or separate roles).'

The word 'Trinity' does not occur in the Bible. It comes from the Latin word *trinitas* coined by Tertullian of Carthage (c. 160-215 A.D.) meaning 'three-ness.' It is a good term to sum up the biblical truth that God is One-in-Three and Three-in-One and it has been freely used in the Christian church from about 220 A.D.

The Bible proclaims but one true God

Monotheism is at the heart of all biblical teaching. Every Jewish child was taught to recite the words of Deuteronomy 6:4, 'Hear, O Israel: The LORD our God, the LORD is one!' It is the central truth of the Old Testament and is reiterated again and again (see Exod. 20:2-3; Deut. 4:35; 1 Kings 8:57,60; Isa. 44:6; 45:5-6; Zech. 14:9).

The New Testament is equally clear about there being only one God. Our Lord Jesus Christ affirmed the words of Moses when someone asked Him, 'Which is the first commandment of all?' to which He replied, 'The first of all the commandments is: "Hear, O Israel, the LORD our God, the LORD is one. And you shall love the LORD your God with all your heart, with all your soul, with all your mind, and with all your strength." This is the first commandment' (Mark 12:29-30). His apostles were also unequivocal in their monotheism. Paul says, 'Therefore concerning the eating of things offered to idols, we know that an idol is nothing in the world, and that there is no other God but one. But even if there are so-called gods, whether in heaven or on earth (as there are many gods and many lords), yet for us there is one God, the Father, of whom are all things, and we for Him; and one Lord Jesus Christ, through whom are all things, and through whom we live' (1 Cor. 8:4-6). Elsewhere he states that 'there is one God who will justify the circumcised by faith and the uncircumcised through faith' (Rom. 3:30; see also 1 Tim. 2:5; James 2:19).

The being of the true God is independent

God is independent of anything whatsoever in creation, because the ground of His existence is solely in Himself. God exists in a different way from us because we,

His creatures, depend on Him for our existence and satisfaction. Our Creator, however, exists in an eternal, self-sustaining, necessary way. We necessarily age and die, because it is part of our present being to do that. God, on the other hand, necessarily continues forever uncaused and unchanged, because it is His eternal nature to do that. 'The idea of God's self-existence,' L. Berkhof points out, 'was generally expressed by the term *aseitas*, meaning *self-originated*, but Reformed theologians quite generally substituted for it the word *independentia* (independence), as expressing, not merely that God is independent in His being, but also that He is independent in everything else: in His virtues, decrees, works, and so on ... As the self-existent God, He is not only independent in Himself, but also causes everything to depend on Him.'[1]

God's self-existence is a basic truth. Paul told the men of Athens that 'God, who made the world and everything in it, since He is Lord of heaven and earth, does not dwell in temples made with hands. Nor is He worshiped with men's hands, as though He needed anything, since He gives to all life, breath, and all things' (Acts 17:24-25; cf. Ps. 94:8ff; Isa. 40:18ff). Again, this self-existence of God is expressed in the divine name God disclosed to Moses when He spoke to him out of the bush that burned steadily without being consumed. The fire did not need to feed on the bush. It was self-existing, a fitting symbol of God. So when Moses asked God what he might tell the Israelites is the name of the God who was sending him to be their deliverer, God first said, 'I am who I am' and then shortened it to 'I am' (Jehovah or Yahweh in Hebrew; Exod. 3:6,13-16). The name proclaims the eternal, self-sustaining, self-

---

1. Berkhof, *Systematic Theology* (Banner of Truth, 1959), p. 58.

determining, supernatural mode of God's existence that the burning bush had symbolized.

THE TRUE GOD IS ONE UNDIVIDED BEING

'The unity of God', says Wayne Grudem, 'may be defined as follows: God is not divided into parts, yet we see different attributes of God emphasized at different times. This attribute of God [His unity] has also been called God's *simplicity,* using *simple* in the less common sense of "not complex" or "not composed of parts". But since the word *simple* today has the more common sense of "easy to understand" and "unintelligent or foolish", it is more helpful now to speak of God's "unity" rather than His *simplicity.*'[2] God is not a complex of parts. He is not a compilation of parts. God is the ultimate, simple, non-complex being, and all He is, He is *synchronously* and not *sequentially.*

As J.I. Packer explains: 'All God's thoughts and actions involve the whole of Him. This is His integration, sometimes called His simplicity. It stands in stark contrast to the complexity and lack of integration of our own personal existence, in which, as a result of sin, we are scarcely ever, perhaps never, able to concentrate the whole of our being and all of our powers on anything. One aspect of the marvel of God, however, is that He simultaneously gives total and undivided attention not just to one thing at a time but to everything and to everyone everywhere in His world past, present and future (cf. Matt. 10:29-30).'[3]

All God's attributes are characteristic of the whole of God's being. So when John says, 'God is light' (1 John 1:5) and then goes on to say, 'God is love' (1 John 4:8,16), he is not asserting that God is partly

---

2. Wayne Grudem, *Systematic Theology,* pp. 177, 178.

3. J.I. Packer, *Concise Theology* (Tyndale House, 1993), pp. 29, 30.

light (holy) and partly love. Nor is he saying that God is more light than love, or more love than light. Nor is he saying that in some situations God must stop being light in order to be love, or stop being love in order to be light. His nature is light, and His nature is no less love. Every attribute of God that we find in Scripture is true of all of God's being, and therefore we can say that every attribute of God also complements every other attribute (cf. Exod. 34:6-7). There are in Him no attributes that can conflict. He cannot be torn different ways by divergent desires. God is one undivided being.

THE OLD TESTAMENT PORTRAYS PLURALITY IN THE ONE GOD

Although there is only one God, the Old Testament portrays a plurality of persons in the Godhead without embarrassment or explanation. Right at the beginning of Scripture, in the story of creation, we read: 'Then God said, "Let Us make man in Our image, according to Our likeness" ... So God created man in His own image; in the image of God He created him; male and female He created them' (Gen. 1:26-27). This is not a 'plural of majesty'. In Old Testament Hebrew there are no other examples of a ruler using plural verbs or plural pronouns of himself in this way. Again, when God spoke these words, He was not talking to the angels! For man was not made in the image of the angels, but in the image of God. The only persons besides the angels that God could have been talking to must be persons in the Godhead.

Likewise in Genesis 3:22 we read, 'Then the LORD God said, "Behold, the man has become like one of Us, to know good and evil."' At the tower of Babel, God, talking to God, says, 'Come, let Us go down and there confuse their language, that they may not understand one another's speech' (Gen. 11:7). Centuries later, Isaiah sees a vision of God in the temple and hears Him saying, 'Whom shall I send, and who will go for Us?' (Isa. 6:8). In all these different events, spread over a few thousand years, only one God is mentioned, and yet He speaks in the plural to other persons whom He regards as equals.

Again, there are passages in the Old Testament where one person is called 'God' or 'the LORD' and is distinguished from another person who is also said to be God. Psalm 45:6-7 says, 'Your throne, O God, is forever and ever ... Therefore God, Your God has anointed You with the oil of gladness more than Your companions' (cf. Heb. 1:8). In Psalm 110:1 David says, 'The LORD said to my Lord, "Sit at My right hand, till I make Your enemies Your footstool."' In Matthew 22:41-46 Jesus points out that David is referring to two separate persons as 'Lord', but who is David's 'Lord' if not God Himself? Jehovah is inviting someone else who is fully God to sit at His right hand, namely Jesus (Acts 2:34-36; Heb. 10:12-13; 12:2). Malachi 3:1-2 is another example: 'The Lord, whom you seek, will suddenly come to His temple ... says the LORD of hosts. But who can endure the day of His coming? And who can stand when He appears?' Once more 'the LORD of hosts', who is the speaker, distinguishes Himself from 'the Lord' who is coming to His temple. These are two separate persons, both of whom can be called 'Lord'.

THE NEW TESTAMENT IDENTIFIES THREE PERSONS AS EQUALLY GOD

The revelation in Scripture of God's person and purposes is progressive revelation. It was not given on one occasion to one person, but gradually revealed by the Holy Spirit through holy prophets at various times over a period of some fifteen hundred years of redemptive history. So the doctrine of the Trinity was not dreamed up after the ascension of Jesus by some disciples who had nothing better to do but speculate about the mysterious being of God. On the contrary, they were Christians whose lives and thinking had been radically impacted by the supernatural events of the birth, life, teaching, miracles, death, resurrection and ascension of Jesus of Nazareth. To quote H.R. Mackintosh, 'Thus in the Bible the idea of God which believers hold, or rather which holds and masters them, has history as its fruitful background and medium ... everything in man's apprehension of God, is as it were lived out in the concrete happenings of time, before being consciously shaped in doctrine.'[4]

For example, the apostles were all Jews, and as Jews they believed tenaciously in one God, whereas the surrounding nations worshipped many gods. This one God was the Creator of the universe who had made a covenant with Israel to have them as His chosen people and bless them. Moreover, Jesus taught them that He was 'the Son of God' who came from heaven and was equal with God the Father, doing and saying the same things that the Father does and says:

> Then Jesus answered and said to them, 'Most assuredly, I say to you, the Son can do nothing of Himself, but what He sees the Father do; for whatever He does, the Son also does in like manner. For the Father loves the Son, and shows Him all things that He Himself does; and He will show Him greater works than these, that you may marvel. For as the Father raises the dead and gives life to them, even so the Son gives life to whom He will. For the Father judges no one, but has committed all judgment to the Son, that all should

---

4. H.R. Mackintosh, *The Christian Apprehension of God* (Student Christian Movement Press, 1934), p.99.

honour the Son just as they honour the Father. He who does not honour the Son does not honour the Father who sent Him' (John 5:19-23). [They are equal.]

For as the Father has life in Himself, so He has granted the Son to have life in Himself, and has given Him authority to execute judgment also, because He is the Son of Man. Do not marvel at this; for the hour is coming in which all who are in the graves will hear His [Christ's] voice and come forth – those who have done good, to the resurrection of life, and those who have done evil, to the resurrection of condemnation (John 5:26-30).

Jesus said to them, 'Most assuredly, I say to you, before Abraham was, I AM' (John 8:58; Jesus is claiming here the divine name 'I AM' revealed to Moses in Exodus 3:13-14 which speaks of God's self-existence).

But although He had done so many signs before them, they did not believe in Him, that the word of Isaiah the prophet might be fulfilled, which he spoke: 'Lord, who has believed our report? And to whom has the arm of the LORD been revealed?' Therefore they could not believe, because Isaiah said again: 'He has blinded their eyes and hardened their hearts, lest they should see with their eyes, lest they should understand with their hearts and turn, so that I should heal them.' These things Isaiah said when he saw His [Christ's] glory and spoke of Him (John 12:37-41).

'If you had known Me, you would have known My Father also; and from now on you know Him and have seen Him.' Philip said to Him, 'Lord, show us the Father, and it is sufficient for us.' Jesus said to him, 'Have I been with you so long, and yet you have not known Me, Philip? He who has seen Me has seen the Father; so how can you say, "Show us the Father"? Do you not believe that I am in the Father, and the Father in Me? The words that I speak to you I do not speak of

My own authority; but the Father who dwells in Me
does the works. Believe Me that I am in the Father and
the Father in Me, or else believe Me for the sake of the
works themselves' (John 14:7-11). [The Father and the
Son are indivisible.]

Jesus answered and said to him, 'If anyone loves Me,
he will keep My word; and My Father will love him,
and We will come to him and make Our home with
him' (John 14:23).

Jesus spoke these words, lifted up His eyes to heaven,
and said: 'Father, the hour has come. Glorify Your
Son, that Your Son also may glorify You, as You have
given Him authority over all flesh, that He should
give eternal life to as many as You have given Him.
And this is eternal life, that they may know You, the
only true God, and Jesus Christ whom You have sent.
I have glorified You on the earth. I have finished the
work which You have given Me to do. And now,
O Father, glorify Me together with Yourself, with the
glory which I had with You before the world was'
(John 17:1-5).

Commenting on John 17:1-5, Sinclair B. Ferguson says:
'Nothing could more clearly underscore Jesus' oneness
with God. He shared His glory; He brings Him glory;
He receives glory from the One who has said, "I will
not give my glory to another" (Isaiah 42:8)'.[5]

By the inspiration of the Holy Spirit, Christ's
apostles, the prophets of the New Testament, endorsed
His teaching by repeating His claims in different ways.
Here are some examples:

In the beginning was the Word, and the Word was with
God, and the Word was God. He was in the beginning
with God. All things were made through Him, and
without Him nothing was made that was made. In

---

5. Sinclair B. Ferguson, *A Heart for God* (Navpress, 1985), p. 35.

Him was life, and the life was the light of men ... And the Word became flesh and dwelt among us, and we beheld His glory, the glory as of the only begotten of the Father, full of grace and truth (John 1:1-4,14).

And after eight days His disciples were again inside, and Thomas with them. Jesus came, the doors being shut, and stood in the midst, and said, 'Peace to you!' Then He said to Thomas, 'Reach your finger here, and look at My hands; and reach your hand here, and put it into My side. Do not be unbelieving, but believing.' And Thomas answered and said to Him, 'My Lord and my God!' (John 20:26-28).

... of whom are the fathers and from whom, according to the flesh, Christ came, who is over all, the eternally blessed God. Amen (Rom. 9:5).

...that at the name of Jesus every knee should bow, of things in heaven, and of those on earth, and of those under the earth, and that every tongue should confess that Jesus Christ is Lord, to the glory of God the Father (Phil. 2:10-11; cf. Isa. 45:23).

For in Him dwells all the fullness of the Godhead bodily (Col. 2:9).

... looking for the blessed hope and glorious appearing of our great God and Savior, Jesus Christ (Titus 2:13).

But to the Son He [God] says, 'Your throne, O God, is forever and ever; a sceptre of righteousness is the sceptre of Your kingdom' ... And: 'You, LORD, in the beginning laid the foundation of the earth, and the heavens are the work of Your hands, they shall perish, but You remain; and they will all grow old like a garment' (Heb. 1:8, cf. Ps. 45:6; Heb. 10-11; cf. Ps. 102:25-27).

'I am the Alpha and the Omega, the Beginning and the End, the First and the Last' (Rev. 22:13; cf. Isa. 44:6).

But there are not just two persons who are God. The Father is God; the Lord Jesus Christ, the Son, is God; and so too is the Holy Spirit. The Holy Spirit is not just the divine power which God exercises in creation and the church. The Holy Spirit is not an 'it' but a 'He', a divine person. This Christian belief is implicit in the following Scriptures:

> The Spirit of God has made me, and the breath of the Almighty gives me life (Job 33:4; cf. Gen. 1:27).

> 'Therefore I say to you, every sin and blasphemy will be forgiven men, but the blasphemy against the Spirit will not be forgiven men (Matt. 12:31-32; the Spirit can be blasphemed because He is God, and we blaspheme Him by rejecting the light of the gospel and remaining impenitent).

> 'I will pray the Father, and He will give you another Helper, that He may abide with you forever ... But the Helper, the Holy Spirit, whom the Father will send in My name, He will teach you all things' (John 14:16,26; see also 15:26; 16:7-10. 'Another Helper', literally translated, is 'another of the same kind', like Jesus).

> But Peter said, 'Ananias, why has Satan filled your heart to lie to the Holy Spirit and keep back part of the price of the land for yourself? While it remained, was it not your own? And after it was sold, was it not in your own control? Why have you conceived this thing in your heart? You have not lied to men, but to God' (Acts 5:3-4; to lie to the Holy Spirit is to lie to God).

> Do you [Christ's church] not know that you are the temple of God and that the Spirit of God dwells in you? (1 Cor. 3:16; cf. 1 Cor. 6:19).

Now the Lord is the Spirit; and where the Spirit of the Lord is, there is liberty (2 Cor. 3:17).

So the Holy Spirit is called God or Lord in the same sense as the Father and the Son. The New Testament identifies all three persons as equally God.

THE THREE PERSONS OF THE GODHEAD ARE DISTINCT BUT NOT SEPARATE

The first indication of this was demonstrated at the baptism of Jesus by John the Baptist in the river Jordan (Matt. 3:13-4:1). First of all, we have God the Spirit descending upon God the Son in the form of a dove (v. 16). Then we have God the Father acknowledging and approving Jesus from heaven with a voice that said, 'This is My beloved Son, in whom I am well pleased' (v. 17). The baptism of Jesus was a Trinitarian event at the very beginning of His ministry. Think also of the end of His life on earth when after His supernatural resurrection, our Lord commissioned His disciples, saying, 'Go therefore and make disciples of all the nations, baptizing them in the name of [not the names of, but in the single name of] the Father and of the Son and of the Holy Spirit' (Matt. 28:19). Here we have our Lord bracketing the three persons of the Godhead together under one name, because they are one God, and yet distinct. The use of the conjunction 'and' is meant to indicate that the Father is not the Son, the Son is not the Holy Spirit, and the Holy Spirit is not the Father. That is an irresistible conclusion from the great commission.

Or take the words in 1 Peter 1:2 where the apostle says that we are 'elect according to the foreknowledge of God the Father, in sanctification of the Spirit, for obedience and sprinkling of the blood of Jesus Christ.' We also have the well-known words of Paul's benediction in 2 Corinthians 13:14, 'The grace of the Lord Jesus Christ, and the love of God, and the communion [fellowship] of the Holy Spirit be with you all.' Again, the conjunction 'and' tells us that we must regard the three as distinct from each other. Paul involves all three persons in his benediction, thereby affirming God's three-ness. He can do this while still maintaining God's one-ness. God is one indivisible essence, but this divine essence exists eternally as the Father, the Son and the Holy Spirit.

THE PERSONS OF THE TRINITY HAVE DIFFERENT PRIMARY FUNCTIONS

In all their activities the three persons are always together and always cooperating, with the Father *initiating*, the Son *complying*, and the Holy Spirit *executing* the will of both, which is His will also. So in the work of creation the Father decreed exactly what He wanted. The Son spoke the word to carry out these creative decrees (John 1:3; Col. 1:16; Heb. 1:2), and the Holy Spirit was active in 'brooding' or 'hovering over the waters' in order to quicken and sustain life (Gen. 1:2; Ps. 139:7). In the work of redemption God the Father planned the way of salvation, chose its subjects, and sent His Son to be their Saviour (John 3:16; Eph. 1:3-11). God the Son obeyed the Father and accomplished redemption for us by coming to earth as a man and offering Himself as a sufficient penal substitutionary sacrifice for the sins of God's people (John 3:14-15; Gal. 3:13; Heb. 10:11-14). God the Holy Spirit was then sent by the Father and the Son to apply redemption to the elect, and complete the work that was planned by the Father and begun by the Son (John 14:26; 15:26; 1 Pet. 1:2).

'Thus', says Wayne Grudem, 'while the persons of the Trinity are equal in all their attributes, they nonetheless differ in their relationships to the creation. The Son and Holy Spirit are equal in deity to God the Father, but they are subordinate in their roles.'[6] Whatever is true about God, is true about each of the three persons of the Trinity, for each of them is fully God and has equal dignity in the Godhead. In this sense no one of them can be either over or under the others. The mystery is that there is but one God who has no other existence except as the three persons of the Trinity. Just as God cannot exist without being omnipotent or omniscient (to take a few of the attributes of His being), so God cannot exist without being 'three personed' (John Donne, 1572-1631).

THE TRINITY IN CHRISTIAN EXPERIENCE

There are many things in life that we find very difficult to explain, but have no difficulty in experiencing. Most of us do not understand electricity, but we experience it every day. The same is true of the emotion of love. We know that it involves a disturbance of the endocrine glands. But what is it? It is something we are not able to explain, yet we can experience it in our daily life. The same is true of the Trinity. Every time we worship and pray as a true Christian, we experience the presence and activity of the Trinity. Paul puts it so clearly in Ephesians 2:18 when he says that 'through Him [Christ] we both [Jews and Gentiles] have access by one Spirit to the Father.' Note the prepositions. We pray *through* Jesus, because He died for our sins to be the mediator between God the Father and us (1 Tim. 2:5). We pray *by* one Spirit, because He is the One who causes us to cry out to God as our Father in heaven and assures us that we are His children (Rom. 8:14-17). And we pray *to* the Father, because He is the One to whom all prayer is to be directed (Matt. 6:6) and who, more than any human father, knows how to

6. Wayne Grudem, *ibid*, p. 249.

give good gifts to His children (Matt. 7:11). We cannot truly pray without being a Trinitarian Christian.

Even when we pray our Lord's pattern prayer, we are affirming our faith in the Trinity. For example, we are instructed to pray for three basic human needs: our daily bread, the forgiveness of our sins and deliverance from evil. These needs are all met by the three persons of the Trinity. Our prayer for *daily bread* is certainly addressed to God the Father because He who feeds the birds, feeds us as well (Matt. 6:26; cf. Acts 14:15-17; 17:25). Our prayer for *forgiveness* is addressed through the Father to God the Son. For there is no possibility of forgiveness for our sins apart from His atoning sacrifice on the cross (Matt. 26:28; Eph. 1:7; 1 Pet. 1:18). Our prayer for *deliverance* from evil is addressed through the Father to God the Holy Spirit, for He is the Helper Jesus sent to give us victory over temptation (Rom. 8:1-2; Gal. 5:16). The Christian Faith is a Trinitarian Faith, and so it is important to always keep in mind the unity of the Godhead. While the three divine Persons have different functions, they are not separate. To worship the Father is to worship the Son and the Holy Spirit. To have the Son dwelling in us is to have the Father and the Holy Spirit dwelling in us as well (John 14:16-18,23).

THE IMPORTANCE OF THE DOCTRINE OF THE TRINITY

Firstly, the doctrine of the Trinity is important for the church's *witness*. The Athanasian Creed says, 'Whosoever wishes to be saved, before all things it is necessary for him to hold the Catholic [Universal] Faith. And the Catholic Faith is this, that we worship one God in trinity, and trinity in unity ... which unless a man shall faithfully and firmly believe, he cannot be saved.' Why? Because the gospel is all about the work of the three persons of the Trinity in our salvation. We must believe that God the Father loves us and gave His Son to save us from perishing in hell (John 3:16). We must believe that the Son bore the punishment of our sins on the cross so that we might be forgiven (Rom. 6:23; 1 Pet. 3:18). And we must believe that we need to be 'born again' of the Spirit to receive eternal life (God's life, John 3:5-7; 2 Pet. 1:1-4). Thus when our Lord Jesus witnessed to Nicodemus, He spoke specifically of these three truths (John 3:16-17; 13-15; 5-8). The doctrine of the Trinity, therefore, requires us to pay equal attention and give equal honour to all three persons in the unity of their gracious saving ministry to us.

Secondly, the doctrine of the Trinity is important for the church's *worship*. The element of mystery is indeed great, but far from being a hindrance to worship, it is actually a help. A God who is far above us fills us with awe and wonder, as it does the hosts in heaven. John says, 'They do not rest day or night, saying: "Holy, holy, holy, Lord God Almighty, Who was and is and is to come!"' (Rev. 4:8). The heavenly host also say, 'You are worthy, O Lord, to receive glory and honour and power; for You created all things, and by Your will they exist and were created' (v. 11). To worship God, one does not need to fully understand His divine being, but simply to believe what He has revealed of Himself in Scripture. How can finite beings comprehend the infinite One?

Thirdly, the doctrine of the Trinity is important to the church's *orthodoxy*. As G.E. Lane explains:

> Any view of God which rejects or even overlooks His three-personal greatness is a poverty-stricken view. It takes the mystery out of His being and reduces Him to near-human terms. We should regard any view which does this as suspect and doomed to extinction. This reduction of God to man-size has been attempted many times in history, but has always failed in the

end. Arianism, Deism, Unitarianism are dead or dying today. We are faced these days with Jehovah Witness-ism. It is lively and strong at present, but it cannot last. The idol-gods are like their makers and always fall. Much teaching about God within the professing Church also today is poverty-stricken … It is not only the sects, but the Church itself that is in danger of following a God of its own making. Let us be sure that our God is the God of the Apostles and Prophets, One perfect and whole Being, expressed in three distinct persons, each fully God.[7]

7. G.E. Lane, *Foundations of the Faith,* p. 10.

3

THE OMNIPRESENCE OF GOD

'Where is God?' is a question often asked by children, and all too often the answer given is with a finger pointing upwards to the sky. We cannot, however, point to any one location and claim that that is where God is. Just as God is unlimited or infinite with respect to time (eternal), so God is unlimited in respect to space. He is omnipresent (the Latin prefix *omni* means 'all'). God is always everywhere present. There is no place anywhere where God is absent. The word *omnipresence* can only be used of God because He alone is eternal and infinite. God is present at every point of space with His whole being to sustain, to bless, or to punish.

THE BIBLICAL TESTIMONY TO GOD'S OMNIPRESENCE

But will God indeed dwell on the earth? Behold, heaven and the heaven of heavens cannot contain You. How much less this temple which I have built! (1 Kings 8:27).

I have set the LORD always before me; Because He is at my right hand I shall not be moved (Ps. 16:8).
Where can I go from Your Spirit?

Or where can I flee from Your presence?
If I ascend into heaven, You are there;
If I make my bed in hell, behold, You are there.
If I take the wings of the morning,
And dwell in the uttermost parts of the sea,
Even there Your hand shall lead me,
And Your right hand shall hold me.
If I say, 'Surely the darkness shall fall on me,'
Even the night shall be light about me;
Indeed, the darkness shall not hide from You,
But the night shines as the day;
The darkness and the light are both alike to You.
For You formed my inward parts;
You covered me in my mother's womb.
I will praise You, for I am fearfully and wonderfully made;
Marvelous are Your works,
And that my soul knows very well.
My frame was not hidden from You,
When I was made in secret,
And skillfully wrought in the lowest parts of the earth.
Your eyes saw my substance, being yet unformed.
And in Your book they all were written,
The days fashioned for me,
When as yet there were none of them (Ps. 139:7-16).

'Am I a God near at hand,' says the LORD,
'And not a God afar off?
Can anyone hide himself in secret places,
So I shall not see him?' says the LORD;
'Do I not fill heaven and earth?' says the LORD
(Jer. 23:23-24).

… so that they should seek the Lord, in the hope that they might grope for Him and find Him, though He is not far from each one of us; for in Him we live and move and have our being, as also some of your own poets have said, 'For we are also His offspring' (Acts 17:27-28).

THE NATURE OF GOD'S OMNIPRESENCE

In the first place we must understand that while God fills all of creation, creation does not contain or confine God's presence. God's omnipresence does not mean that God's presence simply extends to the furthest bounds of space, for space is not boundless, but God is. Space has its limits, God does not. God, being God, is infinite, limitless and boundless. If God is confined to space, He has limits and cannot be infinite. Wherever you have finitude, you have creaturehood, not God. King Solomon was right when he said in his prayer to God, 'Behold, heaven and the heaven of heavens cannot contain You. How much less this temple which I have built!' (1 Kings 8:27). God cannot be confined to anything. God transcends everything. It is an important distinction to make.

Secondly, the nature of God's omnipresence is such that it consists of His Person and not just His power or influence. It is the heresy of Deism that believes that it is only God's power working through natural laws that is in all places all the time. It reduces God to a 'first cause who created this world and instituted immutable, universal laws that preclude any alteration as well as any form of divine immanence.'[1] But God's power cannot be separated from His Person. It is God Himself who is working out His purposes in all places at all times. By the end of the eighteenth century Deism had become a dominant religious view among intellectual Americans like Benjamin Franklin, George Washington and Thomas Jefferson.

Thirdly, the omnipresence of God is not achieved by some distribution of His being. As C. Samuel Storms points out: 'Being wholly spirit, God is not subject to

---

1. M.H. Macdonald, *Evangelical Dictionary of Theology,* edited by Walter A. Elwell (Baker Book House, 1984), p. 305.

the laws of matter such as extension and displacement. He cannot be divided or separated such that one part of His being is here and not there, and another part there and not here. The whole of His being is always everywhere, no less nor more here than there, or there than here.'[2] God is indivisible, and so the whole of His being in all its majesty and power is always present everywhere.

Fourthly, we must, however, be careful not to fall into the error of Pantheism, which identifies God with all of creation, and worships mountains and rivers and beasts and planets like some Eastern religions or followers of the New Age Movement do. God is distinct from all created things, visible or invisible. Although God is present in the totality of His being throughout creation, He is yet distinct from, independent of, and transcendent above all created things (Col. 1:16-17; Acts 17:28). To worship nature is idolatry.

Now if God is in all places at all times, why does the Bible speak of God drawing near to us or abandoning us? Why does Scripture tell us to seek God until we find Him? This raises yet another aspect of the nature of God's omnipresence. God's presence is not to be confused with the manifestation of His presence. For the manifestation of God's presence to us is dependent upon His relationship to us. Thus God's manifestation of His presence in heaven is far greater than it is on earth, for the angels and the saints in heaven are in perfect harmony with God, whereas we are not. The reason we feel that God is remote, is because we have sinned against God and are alienated from Him (Isa. 59:2). God is not remote from us in distance, but He is remote from us in character and favour. It is

---

2. C. Samuel Storms, *The Grandeur of God* (Baker Book House, 1984), p. 89.

like a husband and wife living in the same house, but not on speaking terms. God is there, but we feel cut off from Him because of our sin and rebellion. That is how Jacob felt at Bethel after all his wrongdoing: 'Surely the LORD is in this place, and I did not know it' (Gen. 28:16). It is the presence of God in favour and blessing that makes heaven heaven, and it is the presence of God in judgment and wrath that makes hell the terrible place it is.

THE AWESOMENESS OF GOD'S OMNIPRESENCE

God's omnipresence is awesome in the first place because *it exceeds all dimensions.* This is the theme of Psalm 139 where David extols God's all-embracing knowledge based on His all-encompassing presence. Everything we do and every thought we think is laid bare to the eyes of our ever-present Creator and Judge: 'O LORD, You have searched me and known me. You know my sitting down and my rising up; You understand my thought afar off. You comprehend my path and my lying down, and are acquainted with all my ways. For there is not a word on my tongue, but behold, O LORD, You know it altogether' (vv. 1-4).

David feels he is under the constant surveillance of the all-seeing eyes of God. Not only is his every movement monitored by God, but his inmost thoughts are known as well. Some would feel resentful at such divine scrutiny, but not David. As a believer he knows that God is looking out for him. His reaction is one of gratitude and awe: 'You have hedged me behind and before, and laid Your hand upon me' (v. 5). It is all for David's protection. That is why he goes on to say in verse 6: 'Such knowledge is too wonderful for me; it is high, I cannot attain it.' It is beyond all understanding and all deserving. It is utterly awesome!

In verses 7-10 David explains that God's all-embracing knowledge is based on His inescapable presence. God knows everything precisely because He is everywhere. 'Where can I go from Your Spirit? Or where can I flee from Your presence? If I ascend into heaven, You are there; if I make my bed in hell, behold, You are there. If I take the wings of the morning, and dwell in the uttermost parts of the sea, even there Your hand shall lead me, and Your right hand shall hold me.' There is nowhere that a person can go and be beyond God's help or reach. We could get into a spaceship and be blasted up into the bright blue sky, but we will never out-distance God. Wherever we go, God will be there waiting for us. Nor can we escape God's presence if we travel in the opposite direction. We can descend into the very depths of Sheol or hell, and still not elude God. He is there too! If we travelled in a horizontal direction at the speed of light, whether east or west, we would still not be able to escape from God: 'even there Your hand shall lead me, and Your right hand shall hold me.'

Once again David's reaction is one of wonder and gratitude, for it is a great comfort to all God's people to be assured of God's guiding and protecting hand upon us. No matter how dark the situation may seem to be, God sees as well in the dark as He does in the light. God's guiding and protecting hand is just as reliable in adversity as it is in prosperity: 'If I say, "Surely the darkness shall fall on me," even the night shall be light about me; indeed, the darkness shall not hide from You, but the night shines as the day; the darkness and the light are both alike to You' (vv. 11-12). Or as David puts it in Psalm 23, 'Even though I walk through the valley of the shadow of death [margin: or through the darkest valley], I will fear no evil, for You are with me;

Your rod and Your staff, they comfort me' (v. 4, NIV).
He is the ever-present, inescapable God.

But David is not yet done. If the awesomeness of
God's omnipresence exceeds all dimensions, it also, in
the second place, includes all circumstances, even the
time when he was in the dark depths of his mother's
womb. In an amazing revelation, David says: 'For
You have formed my inward parts; You covered me
in my mother's womb ... My frame was [literally, my
bones were] not hidden from You, when I was made
in secret, and skillfully wrought in the lowest parts
of the earth. Your eyes saw my substance being yet
unformed' (literally 'rolled up' as in a foetal position;
vv. 13,15,16).

David, of course, knew nothing of the details of
human embryology that modern medical science
has discovered, but he knew enough biology to be
amazed at how a human being could be put together
in nine months inside a woman's uterus. He also knew
enough theology to know that the only explanation of
the miracle of life is the activity of God in conception
and confinement. So he says in effect, 'You, O Lord,
were in my mother's womb, weaving all my parts
together, like a weaver blending together different
threads in a complex tapestry. If there was ever a time
when I was concealed in darkness and separated from
You, O Lord, it must surely have been during that
prenatal period of my existence. My mother's womb,
made of dust, was like "the lowest parts of the earth",
and for a time even she was not aware of my existence.
Yet it was precisely then that I was most particularly
the object of Your loving oversight.'

Not only that, David tells us that even before he
was born, God had his life planned for him. 'Your
eyes saw my substance, being yet unformed. And in

71

Your book they all were written, the days fashioned for me, when as yet there were none of them' (v. 16). How awesome is the living God who creates life in the womb, superintending every detail of its development as well as every moment of its subsequent allotted lifespan. And once again David's reaction is not one of resentment, but of grateful wonder: 'I will praise You, for I am fearfully and wonderfully made. Marvellous are Your works, and that my soul knows very well ... How precious also are Your thoughts to me, O God! How great is the sum of them! If I should count them, they would be more in number than the sand; when I awake, I am still with You' (vv. 14,17-18).

The thoughts David has in mind are all the countless details that belong to God's plan for his life; details concerning his parents, his physical and mental and spiritual make-up, his training, his history, and so on. They are so numerous that if he were to diligently count them, he would fall asleep. But upon awaking the counting would have to go on because God would still be with him, and God's plans for him never cease. They continue forever into eternity. No wonder God's thoughts are 'precious' to him. Life is so vulnerable. He needs an ever-present help, and so do we.

Verses 13-16 are of great importance in relation to the whole issue of abortion and the beginning of human life. David, under the inspiration of God, traces the very beginnings of his personal existence, not to the moment of birth, or to some moment of viability, but right back to the moment of conception. When just a foetus, David sees himself as the product of God's creative skills. He is the recipient of God's prenatal care. That may not be the view of some, but it is God's view of the value of prenatal life. The foetus from conception is a human being who is the special focus of God's personal attention. And in the light of that divine truth, nothing can justify treating a foetus as just a part of the mother's body that, like an appendix, she can choose to remove. It has a life of its own with a pulsing heart and all the other members that go to make up a human being. All life, especially human life, owes its origin to the activity of the omnipresent God.

THE PERSONAL EFFECT OF GOD'S OMNIPRESENCE

To believe in an omnipresent God who is in all places at all times has important effects on all human beings. To begin with, it is of tremendous *comfort to God's believing people*. How reassuring it is to know unquestionably that we have a God who is always at our side to help and guide us; a God who cares for us as if we were the sole object of His love and attention. According to our Lord Jesus Christ, God the Father's attention is so detailed that 'the very hairs of [our] head are all numbered' (Matt. 10:30). But even more comforting is the assurance that God's love for His people is committed to saving them from sin for time and eternity. It is a love that is busy all the time working for their good (Rom. 8:28), until at last, by faith and grace, they stand before Him sinless in body and spirit, clothed in the perfect, imputed righteousness of Jesus Christ (2 Cor. 5:21).

No matter what trials God's elect have to go through, His promise is: "'I will never leave you, nor forsake you." So we may boldly say: "The LORD is my helper; I will not fear. What can man do to me?"' (Heb. 13:5-6). And again, 'Thus says the LORD who created you, O Jacob, and He who formed you, O Israel: "Fear not, for I have redeemed you; I have called you by your name; you are Mine. When you pass through the waters, I will be with you; and through the rivers, they shall not overflow you. When you walk through the fire, you shall not be burned, nor shall the flame scorch you"' (Isa. 43:1-2). Paul says, 'For I am persuaded that neither death nor life, nor angels nor principalities nor powers, nor things present nor things to come, nor height nor depth, nor any other created thing, shall be able to separate us from the love of God which is in Christ Jesus our Lord' (Rom. 8:38-39).

In addition to providing comfort, God's omnipresence is also a powerful *incentive for Christian holiness.* As Stephen Charnock comments in his classic treatment of God's attributes:

> What man would do an unworthy action, or speak an unhandsome word in the presence of his prince? The eye of the general inflames the spirit of a soldier. Why did David 'keep God's testimonies'? Because he considered that 'all his ways were before him,' [Ps. 119:168]; because he was persuaded his ways were present with God, God's precepts should be present with him. The same was the cause of Job's integrity: 'doth he not see my ways?' [Job 31:4]; to have God in our eye is the way to be sincere, 'walk before me' as in my sight, 'and be thou perfect,' [Gen. 17:1]. Communion with God consists chiefly in an ordering our ways as in the presence of him that is invisible. This would make us spiritual, raised and watchful in all our passions, if we considered that God is present with us in our shops, in our chambers, in our walks, and in our meetings, as present with us as with the angels in heaven, who though they have a presence of glory above us, yet have not a greater measure of his essential presence than we have.[3]

This is why David separated himself from all evil men. He valued the approval of God far more than the approval of the wicked: 'Oh, that You would slay the wicked, O God! Depart from me, therefore, you

---

3. Stephen Charnock, *The Existence and Attributes of God* (Klock & Klock, 1977), p. 179.

bloodthirsty men. For they speak against You wickedly; Your enemies take Your name in vain. Do I not hate them, O LORD, who hate You? And do I not loathe those who rise up against You? I hate them with perfect hatred; I count them my enemies' (Ps. 139:19-22).

Finally, the effect of God's omnipresence on unbelievers, though still helpful, is one of *discomfort*, because it creates *unease of conscience*. It shatters all those illusions on the basis of which men feel free to sin. Thinking that no one else is around, we steal, or we lie, or we commit adultery, and so on. But what we naively think has been successfully concealed from others, has not been hidden from God. God's word says, 'There is no creature hidden from His sight, but all things are naked and open to the eyes of Him to whom we must give account' (Heb. 4:13). The omnipresent God is a disturbing and threatening God from whose face sinners continually seek to flee and hide, but to no avail. Like Jonah, we may sail to the ends of the earth, but we will never escape from the omnipresent God. If we had any sense, we would not try. David shows us the right way to respond: 'Search me, O God, and know my heart; try me, and know my anxieties; and see if there is any wicked way in me, and lead me in the way everlasting' (Ps. 139:23-24).

Our Creator is not the oppressive tyrant we fear. He cared for us long before we existed. He wove us together in our mother's womb. He has only good thoughts for us. Indeed, the New Testament says, 'For God so loved the world [sinful though we are] that He gave His only begotten Son, that whoever believes in Him should not perish but have everlasting life' (John 3:16). God the Father gave His Son as a sacrifice on the cross for the forgiveness of our sins (Matt. 26:27-28; 1 Pet. 3:18). 'The wages of sin is death, but the gift of God is eternal life in Christ Jesus our Lord' (Rom. 6:23). That is the only way God can deal with 'any wicked way' in us, in order to 'lead [us] in the way everlasting.' Everyone who is willing to be 'searched' by the omnipresent God can claim His promise that 'if we confess our sins, He is faithful and just to forgive us our sins and to cleanse us from all unrighteousness' (1 John 1:9).

4

THE OMNISCIENCE OF GOD

Just as the word *omnipresence* means 'all-present', so the word *omniscience* means 'all-knowing'. In the previous chapter (chapter three) we saw from Scripture that God is all-knowing because He is all-present. He knows everything because He sees everything, and He sees everything because He exists in His total being everywhere. There is no place from which He is absent. Thus David says, 'O Lord, You have searched me and known me. You know my sitting down and my rising up; You understand my thought afar off. You comprehend my path and my lying down, and are acquainted with all my ways' (Ps. 139:1-3; see also vv. 4-12). Solomon, under divine inspiration, echoes the same truth: 'The eyes of the Lord are in every place, keeping watch on the evil and the good' (Prov. 15:3). Both David and his son express themselves figuratively in human terms in order to convey God's omniscience in the most simple and arresting way. Divine truth lies much deeper than finite human minds can comprehend. The Bible writers do this all the time.

But divine omniscience is far greater than knowledge based simply on present observation. Supremely, as we shall see below, it is knowledge based on prior determination, or what Scripture terms 'foreknowledge' or 'foreordination'. In the Greek text it is the same word translated differently according to context (see 1 Pet. 1:2,20). In Peter's first sermon on the Day of Pentecost, the force of the word comes out clearly: 'Men of Israel, hear these words: Jesus of Nazareth ... being delivered by the determined counsel and foreknowledge of God, you have taken by lawless hands, have crucified, and put to death' (Acts 2:22-23). The cause of all things is the will of God. God's omniscience, therefore, has its source both in the eternal, infinite mind and will of God.

THE CHARACTERISTICS OF GOD'S KNOWLEDGE

First of all, it is *infinite*. Job 37:16 asks, 'Do you know the balance of clouds, those wondrous works of Him who is perfect in knowledge?' Psalm 147:5 makes the same claim: 'Great is our LORD, and mighty in power; His understanding is infinite.' There are no degrees of knowledge with God. He does not have to acquire knowledge. He has always known everything there is to know about everything. He never has to update His knowledge, for there is nothing new to God. If there were anything God could learn, it would mean that He did not know it before. If He did not know it before, then He did not know everything; His knowledge would not be perfect and He would not be God. We human beings, because we are finite, are learning all the time. We learn through instruction and study and observation. We can never exhaust the realm of knowledge, but God knows everything absolutely and completely. His knowledge is infinite.

Secondly, God's knowledge is *independent*. He never has to depend on anyone else to fill any possible gaps in His knowledge, for there are none. Thus the prophet Isaiah asks: 'Who has directed the Spirit of the LORD, or as His counsellor has taught Him? With whom did He take counsel, and who instructed Him, and taught Him in the path of justice? Who taught Him knowledge, and showed Him the way of understanding?' (Isa. 40:13-14). To ask the question is to answer it: No-one!

Thirdly, God's knowledge is *infallible*. He is 'perfect in knowledge' (Job 37:16). He never makes a mistake, nor is mistaken. God's understanding of all things is not based upon wrong assumptions which lead to wrong conclusions. God knows everything and everyone perfectly. We make mistakes precisely because we do not know everything. We do things on the assumption that our facts are correct when they are not.

Fourthly, God's knowledge is *eternal*. He never loses any of His knowledge as we do. He remembers everything and forgets nothing. It is true that God has promised, 'I, even I, am He who blots out your transgressions for My own sake; and I will not remember your sins' (Isa. 43:25). But this is not because of some lapse or imperfection on God's part, but a deliberate and loving act of His will not to hold His believing, covenant people accountable. God decides what He is not going to remember, and it is always consistent with His just character. We forget with the passing of time, but God's knowledge is eternal. It neither increases nor decreases.

Fifthly, God's knowledge is *self-determined*. God is totally self-sufficient and self-fulfilled. He had no need to create heaven and earth, and all that is in them. He willed them into being for a wise and good purpose determined beforehand. Before God created anything, He knew precisely what He wanted to do and how it would work out. Nothing was left to chance. Unless God controls everything in creation according to His predetermined plan, He cannot have perfect knowledge and He cannot be omniscient. Things would first have to happen before He could know about them. Scripture references for the self-determined character of God's knowledge will be given below.

THE EXTENT OF GOD'S KNOWLEDGE

If divine omniscience is infinite, which it is, how can we consider its extent? It is limitless! It will help, however, to ponder some of the areas which God's word highlights as being important for His chosen and called people to know and live by.

God has perfect knowledge of Himself

The most important knowledge any being can possess is a true knowledge of himself. The Greeks were the most advanced philosophers of the ancient world, and both Plato and Socrates summed up the purpose of all human study in one simple dictum: 'Man, know yourself!' A person may study a certain branch of learning and become to all intents and purposes an expert in that field. He may become a mathematical genius, but if he does not know himself and what is important for his eternal well-being, he is going to self-destruct. That is the great tragedy in human life today. We only know ourselves to a degree. No one knows himself in a final and absolute sense: 'The heart is deceitful above all things and desperately wicked; who can know it?' (Jer. 17:9). There are sinful traits in our personality that if we fully understood and recognized, we would watch out for – and there would be less addiction, less divorce, less violence and many other evil thoughts and deeds.

God, on the other hand, has a perfect knowledge of Himself. In Matthew 11:27 Jesus says, 'No one knows the Son except the Father. Nor does anyone know the Father except the Son.' The same is true of the Holy Spirit. Paul says in 1 Corinthians 2:11b, 'No one knows the things of God except the Spirit of God.' So each member of the Godhead knows the other members perfectly. There are no unknown imperfections in God, because God is infinitely perfect and holy: 'Therefore you shall be perfect, just as your Father in heaven is perfect' (Matt. 5:48; see also Isa. 6:3; Rev. 4:8). There are no unknown weaknesses in God, because God is infinitely powerful (Ps. 62:11; Jer. 32:17; Luke 1:37). There are no unknown areas where God is lacking in wisdom or love or justice, because God is all-knowing and altogether loving and just (Isa. 40:13-14; 45:21; John 3:16). God, according to Scripture, has perfect knowledge of all His infinite powers and perfections. If He did not, He would be fallible and not God.

God has perfect knowledge of all He has made
Let us start with the universe. Isaiah 40:26 says, 'Lift up your eyes on high, and see who has created these things, who brings out their host by number; He calls them all by name, by the greatness of His might and the strength of His power; not one is missing.' Though there are billions and billions of stars, God decreed their number and He knows each one's name. He does not have to send out a multitude of angels to do a census for Him. But when we come down to the minute things of earth, the knowledge of God is even more staggering. It is easy to imagine God giving His attention to gigantic things like the stars. The earth, however, is not excepted. Isaiah 40:12 tells us that He

'has measured the waters in the hollow of His hand', and so He knows how many gallons the oceans hold. In the same verse, Isaiah says that God has 'calculated the dust of the earth in a measure', and so He knows how many cubic inches it measures and how many tons it weighs.

Our Lord Jesus breaks it down even further when He says: ' Are not two sparrows sold for a copper coin? And not one of them falls to the ground apart from your Father's will ... Do not fear therefore; you are of more value than many sparrows' (Matt. 10:29,31). If the Father watches over every little sparrow and every other little creature right up until the time they die, then He must know everything about them too. Again, in Matthew 10:30, Jesus says, 'The very hairs of your head are all numbered.' What a marvellous example of the infinite knowledge of God! To us every hair is alike, but that is not so with God. He not only knows how many hairs are on each person's head at any time, but He gives each hair a number from the growth of the first to the falling out of the last! God's knowledge of all He has made is infinite. There is no detail in His creation from the greatest things to the smallest, that God does not know perfectly.

God has perfect knowledge of human history
When God created the world, He did not relinquish control of it and allow the forces of evil, whether human or demonic, to take over. Indeed, the reason He created the world is that He has plans for it, and those plans will be worked out to the very last detail. What God has decreed or willed is unstoppable, and so everything that happens in the world comes about by God's good and wise design. If it were possible for something to occur in the world apart from the direct agency or permission of God, then that something

would be independent of God and He would cease to be God. As Daniel 4:35 says, 'He does according to His will in the army of heaven and among the inhabitants of the earth. No one can restrain His hand or say to Him, "What have You done?"'

Another important verse is Isaiah 46:9-10, 'Remember the former things of old, for I am God, and there is no other; I am God, and there is none like Me, declaring the end from the beginning, and from ancient times things that are not yet done, saying, "My counsel shall stand, and I will do all My pleasure."' Or ponder Proverbs 19:21, 'There are many plans in a man's heart, nevertheless the LORD's counsel – that will stand.' According to Scripture, it is God who sets the boundaries of every nation, and dethrones one king for another (Isa. 45:1-7; Dan. 4:32; Acts 17:26). Because the wisdom and power of God are infinite, the accomplishment of whatever He has purposed from the beginning is certain. In history there is no event great or small that may or may not happen. Everything that God has decreed for His glory and creation's good will surely come to pass.

The history of the Bible itself is proof of that. In the Old Testament and the New, predictions concerning the destruction of Jerusalem were made which were fulfilled many years later in the minutest detail (Jer. 29:1-10 and Matt. 24:1-2). Such prophecies could only have been inspired by One who knew the end from the beginning, and whose knowledge rested upon the unconditional certainty of His decrees. Likewise, both the Old Testament and the New contain many prophecies about the return of Christ and the judgement of the world that will be fulfilled to the letter, because God has decreed them (Dan. 7:23-27 and Matt. 24:21-31).

God's knowledge of human history is perfect, not because He is able to foresee the future (which He can), but because He has ordained the future. Thus God knew and foretold the crucifixion of Jesus in Psalm 22, one thousand years before it happened, because it was His will, and the first cause of all things is the will of God. Indeed, the Bible calls Jesus 'the Lamb slain from the foundation of the world' (Rev. 13:8; John 1:29). Before creation it was purposed by God that Jesus should be crucified for our transgressions (Ps. 22; Isa. 53). Hence Peter, speaking of Jesus, says, 'Him, being delivered by the determined counsel and foreknowledge of God, you have taken by lawless hands, have crucified and put to death' and 'For truly against Your holy Servant Jesus, whom You anointed, both Herod and Pontius Pilate, with the Gentiles and the people of Israel, were gathered together to do whatever Your hand and Your purpose determined before to be done' (Acts 2:23; 4:27-28).

Does this mean, then, that we human beings are not free to exercise our own will? that we are mere robots programmed to do God's will? Certainly not! God is not the author of sin. All men and women are free to do what they think will serve their interests best. The problem is that all their desires and plans are selfish and anti-God. They are responsible for what they choose to do. The Jewish priests and Pilate did exactly what they wanted to do when they unjustly crucified Jesus Christ, and yet they carried out God's plan of redemption in doing so. It is a great mystery, but God's sovereignty and man's responsibility are both true facts of human life and history that cannot be denied.

God knows our individual actions and thoughts

O Lord, You have searched me and known me. You know my sitting down and my rising up (Ps. 139:1-2).

O God, You know my foolishness; and my sins are not hidden from You (Ps. 69:5).

You have set our iniquities before You, our secret sins in the light of Your countenance (Ps. 90:8).

The eyes of the LORD are in every place, keeping watch on the evil and the good (Prov. 15:3).

There is no creature hidden from His sight, but all things are naked and open to the eyes of Him to whom we must give account (Heb. 4:13).

More than that, God knows what we are *thinking:* 'You understand my thought afar off ... for there is not a word on my tongue, but behold, O LORD, You know it altogether' (Ps. 139:2,4). When a man is about to speak, he is often ignorant of the exact words that will come from his tongue, but not so with God. Even before a man utters his words, while they are still forming upon his tongue, the Lord knows them 'altogether'. We may be able to hold the words back and conceal the jealousy or hatred in our hearts from others, but we cannot conceal those thoughts from God. As the Bible says:

The LORD searches all hearts and understands all the intent of the thoughts (1 Chron. 28:9).

Thus says the LORD: 'Thus you have said, O house of Israel; for I know the things that come into your mind' (Ezek. 11:5).

But Jesus did not commit Himself to them, because He knew all men, and had no need that anyone should testify of man, for He knew what was in man (John 2:24-25).

THE BLESSING ACCOMPANYING GOD'S OMNISCIENCE

The doctrine of divine omniscience is of great practical benefit in the everyday life of a believer in Jesus Christ. To begin with it should be *a stimulus for joyful worship*. It should fill us with amazement and awe to think of the infinite vastness and intimate detail of God's knowledge of us and of all creation, past, present and future. To think that all our sins were known to God before the world was made, and yet He gave His only begotten Son to die on a cross as an atoning sacrifice for our sins, should fill us with perpetual praise and gratitude. He gave His best for us, knowing our worst. Truly, the realization of all this should bow our hearts in humble wonder and adoration. That is how it affects the saints in heaven who sing a new song: 'You are worthy to take the scroll [of God's purposes] ... for You were slain, and have redeemed us to God by Your blood out of every tribe and tongue and people and nation, and have made us kings and priests to our God; and we shall reign on the earth' (Rev. 5:9-10).

Secondly, an all-knowing God is *a solid ground for Christian comfort*. He can never be surprised or caught off-guard. He knows what is ahead and is fully prepared to bring good out of it, both for Himself and His people. Thus Job could say in the midst of all his terrible losses and suffering: 'He knows the way that I take; when He has tested me, I shall come forth as gold' (Job 23:10). Likewise the apostle Paul affirms: 'We know that all things work together for good to those who love God, to those who are the called according to His purpose' (Rom. 8:28). To quote A.W. Pink: 'The wisdom and power of God being alike infinite, the accomplishment of whatever He hath purposed is absolutely guaranteed. It is no more possible for the Divine counsels to fail in their execution than it would be for the thrice holy God to lie ... There is no future event which is only a mere possibility, that is, something which may or may not come to pass: "*Known* unto God are *all* His works from the beginning" (Acts 15:18). Whatever God has decreed is inexorably certain for He is without variableness or shadow of turning (James 1:17).'[1]

Thirdly, God's omniscience is *a reason for believing prayer*. Life at best is uncertain. We do not know what is coming around the corner. Our wisest action, therefore, is to seek help and guidance from God who is aware of the problems and has the answers. We need never fear being overlooked or having to wait in an endless line of other desperate petitioners. An all-present, all-knowing and all-powerful God is able to give the same attention to one as to all. God's perfect knowledge and power are available to all believers who will seek it in believing prayer. We have His sure word on it: 'It shall come to pass that before they call, I will answer; and while they are still speaking, I will hear' (Isa. 65:24).

Stephen Charnock is very affirming here:

This perfection of God fits him to be a special object of trust. If he were forgetful, what comfort could we have in any promise? How could we depend upon him if he were ignorant of our state? His compassions to pity us, his readiness to relieve us, his power to protect and assist us, would be insignificant, without his omniscience to inform his goodness and direct the arm of his power ... You may depend upon his mercy that hath promised and upon his truth to perform, upon his sufficiency to supply you and his goodness to relieve you, and his righteousness to reward you, because he hath an infinite understanding to know you and your

1. A.W. Pink, *The Attributes of God*, p. 19.

wants, you and your services.[2]

Fourthly, the doctrine of divine omniscience is *an incentive for holy living*. The fact that God sees every deed we do; that nothing escapes His notice, not even the unspoken thoughts of our mind, should be a strong deterrent to sinning and a spur to keep His commandments. How sobering is the knowledge that we can never conceal our sin from the all-seeing eye of God. Adam and Eve were not able to hide their nakedness from God among the trees of the Garden of Eden. No human being saw Cain kill his brother Abel, but God called him to account for it. Examples of God uncovering human sin occur throughout the Bible and substantiate the divine warning: 'Be sure your sin will find you out' (Num. 32:23).

There are other higher incentives for holy living, such as loving obedience to God's holy law and responsive gratitude for the enormous price Jesus Christ paid at Calvary to save us from our sins, but God's omniscience is foundational. As Stephen Charnock reasons:

> This would give check to much iniquity. Can a man's conscience easily and delightfully swallow that which he is sensible falls under the cognizance of God, when it is hateful to the eye of his holiness, and renders the actor odious to him? ... Temptations have no encouragement to come near him that is consistently armed with the thoughts that his sin is booked in God's omniscience ... A sense of God's knowledge of wickedness in the first motion and inward contrivance would bar the accomplishment and execution. The consideration of God's infinite understanding would cry *Stand* to the first glances of the heart to sin.[3]

Finally, God's omniscience is *a call to repentance*

2. Stephen Charnock, *The Existence and Attributes of God*, p. 249.

3. Stephen Charnock, ibid, p. 258.

and faith in God. The natural reaction of unbelieving sinners is to dismiss such a doctrine and resent it as a hostile invasion of a human being's privacy. They may not dismiss the idea of God altogether, but certainly the belief in an all-knowing God. Nobody objects to a non-invasive God, and so the God many people believe in is a figment of their own imagination, a kind of heavenly grandfather who leaves us alone most of the time, but is always there for us when we are in a spot of trouble.

But the omnipresent, omniscient God of the Bible and, in particular, of Psalm 139, will not allow us to reduce Him to a nice comfortable size. Like David, we will find: 'If I make my bed in hell, behold, You are there. If I take the wings of the morning, and dwell in the uttermost parts of the sea, even there Your hand shall lead me' (Ps.139:8-10). God is inescapable. He confronts us wherever we are hiding, insisting on unmasking all those ugly things we would rather keep to ourselves. Moreover, He does this because He loves us. His love is not an *interfering* love, but an *intervening* love. He intervened at Bethlehem in the Person of His Son to take our flesh, and then at Calvary to take away our sin and reconcile us to Himself. He seeks after us because He wants a saving relationship with us that will last for all eternity.

> For the grace [undeserved, unsolicited love] of God that brings salvation has appeared to all men, teaching us that, denying ungodliness and worldly lusts, we should live soberly, righteously, and godly in the present age, looking for the blessed hope and glorious appearing of our great God and Savior Jesus Christ, who gave Himself for us, that He might redeem us from every lawless deed and purify for Himself His own special people, zealous for good works (Titus 2:11-14).

Jesus began His public ministry, with a call to repent of sin and believe the good news of God's salvation: 'The time is fulfilled, and the kingdom of God is at hand. Repent, and believe in the gospel' (Mark 1:15). His apostles echoed the same call.

5

THE WISDOM OF GOD

In giving a separate chapter to God's wisdom we are distinguishing it from His knowledge, but in essence they cannot be separated. God is perfect, lacking in nothing. God's knowledge is all-wise, and His wisdom is all-knowing. These two attributes of God, however, need to be distinguished in our mind in order to give them the proper attention they each deserve if we are to appreciate in some measure the greatness of the living and true God who has revealed Himself in the Bible. In fallen human beings these two mental traits can occur the one without the other. A criminal can have the wits to outsmart the police, but he does so ultimately to his own detriment. A professor may have much learning, but not the wisdom to put it to practical use.

Solomon was the wisest man on earth, but he made a mess of his life with his many wives and his tolerance of idolatry on the part of some (1 Kings 11:4-10). 'In Scripture', says J.I. Packer, 'wisdom is a moral as well as an intellectual quality, more than mere intelligence or knowledge, just as it is more than mere cleverness or cunning. To be truly wise in the Bible sense, one's intelligence and cleverness must be harnessed to a right end. Wisdom is the power to see, and the inclination to choose, the best and highest goal, together with the surest means of attaining it ... As such, it is found in its fullness only in God. He alone is naturally and entirely and invariably wise.'[1] Thus Paul can give praise 'to God, alone wise' and exclaim, 'O the depth of the riches both of the wisdom and knowledge of God! How unsearchable *are* His judgments and His ways past finding out!' (Rom. 16:27; 11:33).

GOD'S WISDOM IS IMPLEMENTED BY HIS ALMIGHTY POWER

Human wisdom can be checked by obstacles or forces beyond its control. Parents may advise their child against harmful behaviour and be ignored. Much failure and suffering in life is due to the rejection of wise counsel. God's wisdom, however, never fails, because it is always enacted by His infinite power. God infallibly implements all His wise decrees. Thus in Scripture divine wisdom and divine power are often linked: 'God is wise in heart and mighty in strength' (Job 9:4; see also 28:20-28). When God gave the interpretation of Nebuchadnezzar's dream to Daniel, the prophet 'answered and said, "Blessed be the name of God forever and ever, for wisdom and might are His"' (Dan. 2:20). God's almighty wisdom is behind all His plans for the world, and so He wonderfully achieves all His objectives. Such a God is to be trusted implicitly with carrying out all His goals and fulfilling all His promises. Nothing He does can be improved. Like Him, His works are perfect.

What then is God's plan for the world? Why did He create the angels, the universe and the human race in

---

1. J.I. Packer, *Knowing God* (Hodder and Stoughton, 1973), p. 80.

the first place? As has been pointed out in the previous chapters, it was not because He needed their company or worship. The perfect fellowship and felicity and adoration within the eternal and infinite Godhead cannot be augmented. Divine perfection cannot be improved. Rather God's purpose was what it always has been and will be: namely, the manifestation of His glory. In His grace and generosity God decreed to manifest His glory to, in and through creation for all eternity. When Adam and Eve disobeyed God and plunged the world into a fallen state, God's plan did not change.

Indeed, what the devil meant for evil, God meant for good. God is still carrying out His original plan to have a people for Himself who will rejoice forever before His glory (John 1:29; Rev. 7:9-17). Moreover, He is redeeming them in such a manner as to make them pocket their pride, loathe their sins, and glorify Him for His mercy, recognising that their salvation is wholly of His grace and not their own doing. In this way, God's grace makes the glory of God a richer thing in the eyes of all creation than it would have been if man had never sinned. For God's redeemed people now have His grace in redemption as well as His goodness in creation for which to give Him thanks and praise. This was the plan God in His infinite wisdom chose as the noblest way to secure His highest glory in the world. And every step in the process of man's salvation has been planned by that same wisdom, with that same end in view. Everything serves to humble man as a sinner and exalt God as man's all-wise Saviour. Every part of the Bible, rightly read, tells us that God's purpose is to manifest His glory in and through the eternal salvation of sinners whom He has graciously brought to repentance and faith in Christ, His Son.

GOD WISDOM IS NOW BEING MADE KNOWN TO MEN AND ANGELS

This is the theme of Ephesians 3. It is all about 'the mystery of Christ' (v. 4) to fulfil God's eternal plan to create His church, the assembly of believing followers 'chosen ... to be a people for Himself, a special treasure above all the peoples on the face of the earth' (Deut. 7:6; cf. Eph. 1:3-6; 1 Pet. 2:9-10). This mystery (or secret) 'which in other ages was not made known to the sons of men', Paul says, 'has now been revealed by the Spirit to His holy apostles and prophets' (v. 5). By their preaching of the gospel, and the church's since then, this former mystery is now no longer a hidden secret. Paul had a significant role, under God's sovereign plan, in making this new revelation known to Jews and Gentiles: 'To me, though I am the very least of all the saints, this grace was given, to preach to the Gentiles the unsearchable riches of Christ, and to bring to light for everyone what is the plan of the mystery hidden for ages in God, who created all things' (vv. 8-9, ESV).

But God's purpose went further than that! In verse 10 Paul says that it is also God's 'intent that now the manifold wisdom of God might be made known by the church to the principalities and powers in the heavenly places.' The words 'principalities and powers' refer to that invisible realm in which both holy and fallen angels are engaged in spiritual conflict (Eph. 1:3; 6:12). The theatre of this world is not big enough for the proclamation of 'the eternal purpose which He accomplished in Christ Jesus our Lord' (v. 11). God intends for all the angelic beings in the heavenly places to see the glory of His manifold wisdom in the creation of the fellowship of Christ's church.

For fallen angels it brought shock and dismay. When the Son of God was crucified and buried, the demons and Satan believed they had foiled God's plan of redemption. The whole human race was doomed to perish with them in hell forever. But when Jesus rose from the grave on the third day, their premature shouts of triumph ended in a deafening silence. The wisdom of God in Christ crucified was manifestly clear and Satan tasted bitter defeat. Moreover, his mission to create strife and turmoil in the world began to be undone. 'Only then', says C. Leslie Mitton, 'as God's reconciling power in Christ became effective in his Church and produced a united fellowship out of elements which in the world had seemed irreconcilable, did the powers of evil realize what God was achieving. Their purpose had been to foster strife and division among men. Now they saw at work a force powerful enough to neutralize their evil intentions and bring peace.'[2]

On the other side, the rejoicing and celebrating has never stopped, nor ever will. God's holy angels and His redeemed people in heaven and on earth now have the highest cause for which to praise Him; a wisdom so great that it achieves what seemed morally impossible. God devised a just way to forgive penitent, believing sinners by bearing the penalty of their sin in the Person of His dear Son (2 Cor. 5:18-21). That is why Jesus Christ is now the focal point of all worship in heaven (Rev. 7:9-10). So it should be for every man and woman on earth, not just for Christians. But, alas, it is not! How terrible is the apathy of the unconverted to the gospel. Think of the things that excite people in the world today, and compare their utter worthlessness to the sight of believers gathered into one multi-national, multi-cultural family, rejoicing in God's redeeming love set upon them from all eternity; and the sight of God rejoicing in the love of His people evoked

---

2. C. Leslie Mitton, *Ephesians* (Wm. B. Eerdmans,1983), p. 127.

by His grace made known through the gospel. The indifference of the world greatly compounds their sin. How far fallen is humankind when we can be moved by trifles, and not care anything for the things that will fill heaven with joy for the rest of eternity. It is God's will, says our text, that throughout the entire universe 'His manifold wisdom might be made known by the church' (v. 10). That is to say, by its fruit in Christ's church. For all creation, men and angels, will worship the wisdom of God which is never at a loss to carry out His purposes whatever the problems encountered in redeeming a ruined race.

GOD'S WISDOM IS SEEN SUPREMELY IN CHRIST'S CHURCH

That is how I think the words 'might be made known by the church' should be understood. God means the church that His Son is building (Matt. 16:18) should be the greatest proof and object-lesson of His wisdom for all eternity. To be sure, His wisdom is also to be seen in *creation*. Thus Paul speaks in verse 9 of the 'God who created all things through Jesus Christ.' For anyone with eyes to see, it is a world of awe and wonder in which one can find ceaseless cause for glowing admiration and heartfelt praise of God's handiwork. Thus the psalmist cries out, 'O LORD, how manifold are Your works! In wisdom You have made them all. The earth is full of Your possessions' (Ps. 104:24). Again, David says, 'I will praise You, for I am fearfully and wonderfully made; marvellous are Your works, and that my soul knows very well' (Ps. 139:14).

Paul, however, is saying in Ephesians 3:10 that if we want to see the true greatness of God's many-splendoured wisdom, we must look at His *new creation*, the church (2 Cor. 5:17). For the church is the place where 'the only wise God' (Jude 25, KJV) has brought together things that otherwise could never have been united. Take our Lord Jesus Christ first. He is the Head of the church. The church is His body. He is the One to whom the church belongs. And what does Paul say of Christ? He says in verse 9 that Jesus Christ is the Creator of all things. In verse 11 he says that Jesus Christ is 'our Lord'. He is our sovereign God, because the title 'Lord' is the same title given to Jehovah in the Greek translation of the Old Testament (Acts 2:21, cf. Joel 2:32; Phil. 2:9-11, cf. Isa. 45:22-23). And because Jesus is God, Paul says in verse 8 that He is the possessor of 'unsearchable riches'. In Colossians 2:9 the apostle puts it more directly when he says, 'In Him [Christ] dwells all the fullness of the Godhead bodily.'

But in order to create the church, God in His wisdom united His divine nature in Christ to our human nature. He sent us a Saviour who is both God and man (1 Tim. 3:16). He needed to be both to save us, and this could only have happened through the miraculous conception of Jesus in the womb of the virgin Mary. He was conceived by the Holy Spirit and not by a human father (Matt. 1:19-23; Luke 1:31-35). It is impossible to explain or understand, but then infinite wisdom is unsearchable. Thus Paul says in 1 Timothy 3:16, 'Great is the mystery of godliness: God was manifested in the flesh.' In that act God, in His wisdom, combined two opposites: the finite and the infinite to be our Saviour.

But there is more! In the second place, Paul also tells us in this letter that God in His wisdom has united men who are sinful to Himself who hates sin and cannot bear to look at it (Hab. 1:13). How did God do that? We must never tire of answering: He did it by taking the guilt of our sin upon Himself and dying in our place on the cross. God suffered for the sins of His people at Calvary, and so Paul says, 'But now in Christ Jesus you who once were far off [because of our sin] have been made near by the blood of Christ' (Eph. 2:13), and have become 'a dwelling place of God' (Eph. 2:22). Or as Paul says in 2 Corinthians 5:19,21: 'God was in Christ, reconciling the world to Himself, not imputing their trespasses to them ... For He made Him who knew no sin to be sin for us, that we might become the righteousness of God in Him.' In this incredible way divine wisdom in Christ solved the problem that divine justice presented, and thereby reveals its unsurpassed greatness. That is why Jesus said, 'There is joy in the presence of the angels of God over one sinner who repents' (Luke 15:10). They rejoice at the wisdom that has opened for sinful men a way back to God that otherwise would never have existed.

God's wisdom in the means He uses to advance His church

Who would have thought that the only wise God would have chosen the preaching of men as the means of declaring the creation of a new humanity, a new society for Himself? He could have used the superior gifts and dazzling appearance of angels to do the job. Why then does He use ordinary human beings instead? This never ceased to amaze the apostle Paul. He says in verse 8, 'To me, who am less than the least of all the saints, this grace was given, that I should preach among the Gentiles the unsearchable riches of Christ.' In 2 Corinthians 4:7 Paul says that Christians have the treasure of the gospel message 'in earthen vessels, so that the excellence of the power may be of God and not of us.' In 1 Corinthians 1 he puts it in even starker terms. He says, 'God has chosen the foolish things of the world to put to shame the wise; and God has chosen the weak things of the world to put to shame the things which are mighty; and the base things of the world and the things which are despised God has chosen, and the things which are not, to bring to nothing the things that are, that no flesh should glory in His presence' (vv. 27-29). It is the glory of God's wisdom that Christ should build His church through the preaching of ordinary redeemed human beings who can never take the credit for it; 'as it is written, "he who glories, let him glory in the Lord"' (1 Cor. 1:31).

GOD'S WISDOM IS PROVED BY THE FACT THAT HIS PURPOSES NEVER CHANGE

What is it that proves that our human wisdom is so limited? Is it not the fact that we have to continually adjust our plans? And the reason we have to revise them is that there are many unforeseen circumstances that arise and force us to make corrections even to our best thought-out plans. God, on the other hand, never has to do that, because He is infinitely wise. He never has to adjust or change His plans, because He purposed all things from the beginning. That is what Paul is referring to in verse 11 when He speaks of 'the eternal purpose which God accomplished in Christ Jesus our Lord'. He is saying that God's purpose for the church to exhibit His manifold wisdom to men and angels cannot fail, because it was planned and ordained in eternity long before the world began, and what God plans is always carried out. Our Lord therefore said, 'I will build My church, and the gates of Hades shall not prevail against it' (Matt. 16:18).

Paul had the same confidence. He was writing from a prison in Rome to his converts in Ephesus who were fearful that his possible execution would be a serious setback to God's cause. What would become of the church if Paul died? So he says in verse 13, 'Therefore I ask that you do not lose heart at my tribulations for you.' Why not? Because it is for 'your glory'. Paul's imprisonment was not pointless. The letter he was writing to them would bring incalculable blessing to them and many others down the years until the return of Christ. God's plans for His church were laid out in eternity and nothing can change them. His purpose will be accomplished regardless. He was 'the prisoner of Jesus Christ' (3:1). He was not the prisoner of circumstances. Indeed, in his letter to the Philippians he tells them of another benefit of his imprisonment for the gospel. He says, 'I want you to know, brethren, that the things which happened to me have actually turned out for the furtherance of the gospel, so that it has become evident to the whole palace guard, and to all the rest, that my chains are in Christ; and most of the brethren in the Lord, having become confident by my chains, are much more bold to speak the word without fear' (1:12-14).

It is important that we never lose sight of the truth that the church exists for God's glory. It is very sad when people speak as if the church existed purely for their comfort and benefit. They measure a church by their immediate needs. Is this a church that makes me feel good? Will my children find friends or a spouse in this congregation? How self-centred! The church exists to display 'the manifold wisdom of God' (literally, the multi-coloured, multi-faceted wisdom of God). It is like a flawless diamond as big as the earth, with so many facets that not even the angels can take in all the many colours that are reflected from it. Each colour shows but a tiny part of the glory of God's wisdom in planning the salvation of His redeemed people. God's angels have been surveying the world since human history began (1 Pet. 1:12) but nothing like this occurred before Calvary, nor anything like it since.

Do we belong to Christ's worldwide, eternal church which has been the central object of God's attention from the very beginning of time? Have we come to Jesus Christ for the forgiveness of our sins? This is the most important thing that can happen to us; that the outworking of 'God's manifold wisdom' in the salvation of our sinful and wretched souls, should be the contemplation of every human and angelic being, not just for a moment, but for all eternity! Our earthly accomplishments (our riches, or degrees, or our successes on the screen or on the sports field) will not be the object of such contemplation. But our salvation will! Our membership of the body of Christ will! Let us take Jesus Christ as our Saviour now, and let Him make us just one facet of God's multi-coloured wisdom. This will keep the courts of heaven ringing forever and ever with the praises of those whose hearts overflow in responsive, grateful love to Him.

> Now to Him who is able to do exceedingly abundantly above all that we ask or think, according to the power that works in us, to Him be glory in the church by Christ Jesus to all generations, forever and ever. Amen (Eph. 3:20-21).

6

THE OMNIPOTENCE OF GOD

Martin Luther once said to Erasmus, who was a humanist (a devotee of reason): 'Your thoughts of God are too human.' This is a natural failing of all human beings whose minds have not been enlightened by God's revelation of Himself in the Bible. Instead of thinking God's thoughts after Him, we shape our thoughts of God after ourselves, and find it hard to believe that God is not in some sense weak and limited as we are. But the God of the Bible is infinite and unlimited in every part of His being. He is not only omnipresent (everywhere present), and omniscient (all-knowing), He is also omnipotent or all-powerful. This theological term, like the first two, is a conjugation of two words: *omnis* meaning all, and *potent* meaning power. The adjective *omnipotent* occurs only once in the Bible, in Revelation 19:6, where it is used to describe God: 'Alleluia! For the Lord God omnipotent reigns!' (literally, the Lord God all-powerful).

However, the concept of a God who is all-powerful or almighty is found throughout Scripture. The word 'almighty' occurs fifty-six times and is used only of

God. The following verses are just a few references to God's omnipotence:

> When Abram was ninety-nine years old, the LORD appeared to Abram and said to him, 'I am Almighty God; walk before Me and be blameless' (Gen. 17:1).

> 'I appeared to Abraham, to Isaac, and to Jacob, as God Almighty' (Exod. 6:3).

> But our God is in heaven; He does whatever He pleases (Ps. 115:3).

> 'Behold, I am the LORD, the God of all flesh. Is there anything too hard for Me?' (Jer. 32:27).

> But Jesus looked at them and said to them, 'With men this is impossible, but with God all things are possible' (Matt. 19:26; cf. Gen. 18:14; Jer. 32:17,27).

> The four living creatures, each having six wings, were full of eyes around and within. And they do not rest day or night, saying: 'Holy, holy, holy, Lord God Almighty, Who was and is and is to come!' (Rev. 4:8).

But the best-known passage in the Bible of God's Almighty power is surely Isaiah 40 where the prophet seeks to comfort the Jews who in less than one hundred years would be exiled in Babylon and need to be reminded of God's great power. They would feel that their situation was hopeless; that they would never be free again to enjoy life in the land God had promised them. Isaiah, under divine inspiration, knew that they would need a new vision of God's infinite power, and so he exhorts them to look at creation to impress upon them that He is almighty. Indeed, God's power is so great that even the mightiest things of creation 'before Him are as nothing, and they are counted by Him less than nothing and worthless' (v.17). Isaiah 40 is a magnificent treatise on the omnipotence of God, and we can break it down into four main concepts.

GOD'S POWER IS SUPREME

Here are some of the illustrations the prophet uses. In verse 12 he looks at the world of nature. He says, 'Who has measured the waters in the hollow of his hand, measured heaven with a span [literally, the width of His hand] and calculated the dust of the earth in a measure? Weighed the mountains in scales and the hills in a balance?' Only God can hold all the water of the seas in the hollow of one hand. Only God's hand is big enough to span the heavens. Only God can pick up all the dust of the earth including the mountains and the hills, and weigh them in a scale pan.

'Behold, the nations', says Isaiah, they 'are as a drop in a bucket, and are counted as the small dust on the scales ... all nations before Him are as nothing and they are counted by Him as less than nothing and worthless' (vv. 15, 17). Israel at this time lived with the great imperial powers of Assyria and Babylon and Egypt ready to sweep over her, making her feel like the little dwarf nation she really was. Who could deliver her and protect her from these giant super-powers? God can, says Isaiah. They may be like a flood ready to carry Israel away, but for God, the disposal of all the nations would be as easy as emptying out a drop of water that remains at the bottom of a bucket. That is all they are before His almighty power. China today may have two million combat troops as well as a ballistic missile system capable of hitting any city in the world; but they are no match for God.

In verses 18-20, Isaiah compares Israel's God to the gods of the heathen, and here he can only be contemptuous. Can you really compare God with the images they have made with their own hands and overlaid with gold, and which have to be secured by silver chains so that they 'will not totter'? It is an insult to God the Creator to equate them with Him. Their human creators cannot give them life or power to move and do things. Or consider the 'princes' of men who are revered by their people as gods. They may be mighty generals or emperors, but 'He [God] brings the princes to nothing; He makes the judges [rulers] of the earth useless. Scarcely shall they be planted; scarcely shall they be sown; scarcely shall their stock take root in the earth, when He will also blow on them and they will wither, and the whirlwind will take them away like stubble' (vv. 23-24). So easily can God dispose of this world's tyrants! They do not compare with Him.

Do not even compare Him, says Isaiah, to the brilliant stars in the sky: 'Lift up your eyes on high, and see who has created these things, who brings out their host by number; He calls them all by name [though there are billions of them], by the greatness of His might and the strength of His power; not one of them is missing.' Lift up your eyes and look at the universe of universes. Here is vastness indeed. Here is power and glory beyond man's comprehension. But alas, familiarity has bred contempt! The philosopher Kant once said, 'If all the stars appeared on one night each century, then men would believe and tremble.' He may well be right. If we are looking for something that will stretch our conception of the power of God to the limit, we only need to look at the stars. The more we find out about them, the more mind-boggling they become. The nearest star is hundreds of millions of miles away, and the temperature of a minor one is at least fourteen million degrees centigrade, and there are billions in every galaxy. Yet even the stars only give us the barest glimmering of what God's power is like. It is infinite and eternal. It cannot be restrained, or confined, or limited in any way, by anyone.

For a theological definition of divine power, Stephen Charnock is old-fashioned in his language, but superb in his insight:

> The power of God is that ability and strength whereby he can bring to pass whatsoever he please, whatever his infinite wisdom can direct, and whatsoever the infinite purity of his will can resolve ... The power of God gives activity to all the other perfections of his nature, and is of a larger extent and efficacy, in regard of its objects, than some perfections of his nature ... How vain would be his eternal counsels, if power did not step in to execute them? His mercy would be a feeble pity, if he were destitute of power to relieve; and his justice a slighted scare-crow, without power to punish; his promises an empty sound, without power to accomplish them. As holiness is the beauty, so power is the life of all his attributes in their exercise; and as holiness, so power is an adjunct belonging to all, a term that may be given to all. God hath a powerful wisdom to attain his ends, without interruption. He hath a powerful mercy to remove our misery: a powerful justice to lay all misery upon offenders; he hath a powerful truth to perform his promises; an infinite power to bestow rewards and inflict penalties. It is to this purpose power is first put in the two things which the psalmist had heard: Ps. lxii. 11, 12, 'Twice have I heard,' or 'two things have I heard;' first power, then mercy and justice included in that expression, 'Thou renderest to every man according to his work.' In every perfection of God he heard of power. This is the arm, the hand of the Deity, which all his other attributes lay hold on, when they would appear in their glory; this hands them to the world, by this they act, in

this they triumph. Power framed every stage for their appearance in creation, providence, redemption.[1]

GOD'S POWER HAS NO LIMITS EXCEPT THOSE SET BY HIS HOLY WILL

Isaiah makes the point in verse 28 that God's power can never be exhausted: 'Have you not known? Have you not heard? The everlasting God, the LORD, the Creator of the ends of the earth, neither faints nor is weary.' God did not stop His work of creation on the sixth day because He was weary or tired. He could have created much more than He did, if He so pleased. Rather, He stopped because He had created everything He purposed to create for His glory. His will set the limits to what He created. Psalm 135:6 says, 'Whatever the LORD pleases He does, in heaven and in earth, in the seas and in all deep places.' But it does not please God to act contrary to His nature and deny Himself (2 Tim. 2:13). Thus Hebrews 6:18 says that 'it is impossible for God to lie.' To quote Charles Hodge, 'It degrades God to suppose that He can be other than He is, or that He can act contrary to infinite wisdom and love. When, therefore, it is said that God is omnipotent because He can do whatever He wills, it is to be remembered that His will is determined by His nature. It is certainly no limitation to perfection to say that it cannot be imperfect.'[2] Although God's power is infinite, His use of that power is always consistent with His character which is perfectly holy and loving.

If God's power operates according to His will, which it always does, that means that the exercise of His power is optional. Before creation, in the long ages of eternity past, God had no need to create

1. Stephen Charnock, *The Existence and Attributes of God*, pp. 364, 366.

2. Charles Hodge, *Systematic Theology* (Wm. B. Eerdmans, 1970), I:409.

anything. Although divine power is of the essence of God, it is not necessary that He always exercises His power. Moreover, when God does exercise His power according to His will, it can be done either by appointed means (second causes), or without appointed means (by Himself as the first cause). When God uses second causes, He manifests His power through things He has already created: that is, through angels or men or nature. When God works without appointed means through Himself as the first cause, He operates by divine fiat: that is, through miracles such as the creation of the universe out of nothing by His spoken word (Ps. 33:6,9). The regeneration of a believing sinner is another example (John 3:3-7; 2 Cor. 5:17).

GOD'S POWER REQUIRES NO MEANS EXCEPT HIS SPOKEN WORD

Our power almost always requires *means*. We need something or somebody to exercise power. We need electricity for light, or gas for heat, or a shovel to dig, and so on. But God needs no means at all. According to the Bible, God only has to command what He wills and it is done. He needs no means beyond His spoken word: 'In the beginning God created the heavens and the earth ... Then God said, "Let there be light"; and there was light' (Gen. 1:1,3, see also v. 9). The psalmist confirms this, saying, 'By the word of the LORD the heavens were made, and all the host of them by the breath of His mouth ... For He spoke and it was done. He commanded, and it stood fast' (Ps. 33:6,9). God says in Isaiah 55:11, 'So shall My word be that goes forth from My mouth. It shall not return to Me void, but it shall accomplish what I please, and it shall prosper in the thing for which I sent it.' Hebrews 11:3 picks up the same theme: 'By faith we understand that the worlds were formed by the word of God, so that the things which are seen were not made out of things which are visible.' God made the world out of nothing and without any help. He required no means except His spoken word to accomplish His will.

It is not until we have to some extent felt, imagined and wrestled with these dimensions of power that we can say we know something of the God of the Bible. Until we get our minds just a fraction around God's omnipotence, we are always going to have thoughts of God that are too human. The living and true God of the Bible is a God of almighty, infinite power that has no limits except those set by His own will and who only has to speak in order for His will to be done. It is sobering to contemplate. If we are honest, there is something rather terrifying about a power like that. We see power abused on every hand, not only by criminals, but also by people in authority. So it should make us a little apprehensive to think that there is such unparalleled power in the world that is not under our control. What if it were turned against us? Does God's word have something else to say that can be of reassurance to us? It does!

GOD'S POWER IS PERSONAL, NOT IMPERSONAL

It is very important to understand and recognise this, because there are other religions in the world who believe in a supreme Being, like Muslims. But Allah is not the living and true God of the Bible. Allah is a god of arbitrary force and callous tyranny. Whatever happens in life is a matter of mechanical fate for Muslims. There is no *love* or *reason* behind it. But the God of the Bible, the God and Father of our Lord Jesus Christ, is both almighty and personal, and that means He is not only to be *feared*, but to be *trusted*.

The story of Noah and the great flood in Genesis 6 to 9 brings this out very clearly. That worldwide catastrophe is introduced in this way: 'Then the LORD saw that the wickedness of man was great in the earth, and that every intent of the thoughts of his heart was only evil continually. And the LORD was sorry that He had made man on the earth, and He was grieved in His heart. So the LORD said, "I will destroy man whom I have created from the face of the earth, both man and beast, creeping things and birds of the air; for I am sorry that I have made them." But Noah found grace in the eyes of the LORD' (Gen. 6:5-8). The fact that God decided to destroy the whole world at a stroke is very frightening indeed. But the Bible does not give us that picture of God to throw us into such a terrified state that we lose all thought of putting our trust in Him. For the Bible is careful to inform us that the power that God wielded there was not arbitrary and mechanical and callous. On the contrary, it is personal. That means it is moral and rational and caring. All of these characteristics of God's power are reflected in the story of the great flood.

To begin with, it was a *moral* display of power, because it was the sight of the great wickedness of men on the earth that moved God to exercise His power in this way. It was not just an arbitrary decision on the part of God to suddenly destroy the world. There was nothing capricious about it. It was a response to such a grave moral decline in the behaviour of men and women that God says 'every intent of the thoughts of his heart was only evil continually.' That is why the decree went out to destroy the world. Moreover, it was *rational*, for God first thought about it and then said to Himself, 'I will destroy man whom I have created.' The book of Genesis does not portray to us some kind of mechanical force that just destroys things without any real purpose or intelligence. Rather, God is portrayed here as a self-conscious being who thinks about what He is going to do. He has a plan in His mind, and although it involves destruction, it is a rational plan.

Perhaps, most important of all, we see a *caring* purpose behind this terrifying display of power. For we read, 'And the LORD was sorry that He had made man on the earth, and He was grieved in His heart.' That is an extraordinary statement. Have we ever thought that God is not only angered by our sin, but grieved and hurt over it? Grief is a symptom of love, and every true parent feels that grief when the child they brought into the world becomes a murderer or a rapist or a terrorist. How much greater, then, is the hurt the infinite God feels? The God of the Bible is not a God who sits in heaven emotionally removed from the people He has created, but a God who is affected by our sin. He is grieved by it, just as Jesus was grieved at the sin of Jerusalem and wept over the city on the Sunday before they crucified Him (Luke 19:41-44; see also 13:34-35). Metaphorically speaking, when God judges men, it is with tears in His eyes. He is grieved by their sin.

But there is another evidence of God's love and caring in this story of the flood, and it is to be seen in the fact that God makes *promises* that can be trusted. For at the end of the story in Genesis 8:21-22 we read, 'Then the LORD said in His heart, "I will never again curse the ground for man's sake, although the inclination of man's heart is evil from his youth; nor will I again destroy every living thing as I have done. While the earth remains, seedtime and harvest, cold and heat, winter and summer, and day and night shall not cease."' And then again in Genesis 9:11-12, God says, '"Thus I establish My covenant with you. Never again shall all flesh be cut off by the waters of the flood; never again shall there be a flood to destroy the earth." And God said: "This is the sign of the covenant which I make between Me and you, and every living creature that is with you, for perpetual generations: I set My rainbow in the cloud, and it shall be for the sign of the covenant between Me and the earth."'

What a comfort and assurance that promise to Noah must have been! Can you imagine how nervous he must have been when he set foot out of the ark on dry land again? After all, he had just witnessed the greatest display of power ever seen by man first-hand. He had seen the whole human race and every living creature eradicated. No nuclear holocaust today could ever eliminate the entire population of the world more successfully. So how was he to know when he began a new life on the earth that this all-powerful God would not do something similar in the near future? If we put ourselves in Noah's shoes, I am sure we would also feel a little nervous to know that there was an almighty God like that watching us. How could anyone cope with such uncertainty? The answer is that when Noah stepped out of the ark God gave him a promise, and a promise is a commitment to act predictably. That is why they are so important in marriage. We have promises in a marriage because they remove doubt and fear from our minds. Without the promise to love and to cherish the other till death do us part, we would always be wondering: Suppose he stops loving me? Suppose she finds somebody else? That is why God gave this promise to Noah. He was saying: You can trust Me, because you can rely on My word. I will never destroy the world again by means of a flood.

The God of the Bible can be trusted in spite of the omnipotent power He has, because of His *character*.

He is a moral, rational and caring God; and, most especially, because of His great care for us we know that He will use His power in accord with the promises He has made to us. Indeed, this is what ultimately secures our belief in the God of the Bible. It is because He has made a covenant with all who will put their trust in Him. On the night before He died on the cross, God in Christ took the red wine and said, 'This is My blood of the new covenant, which is shed for many for the remission [forgiveness, mg.] of sins. But I say to you, I will not drink of this fruit of the vine from now on until that day when I drink it new with you in My Father's kingdom' (Matt. 26:28-29; cf. 2 Cor. 5:18-21).

One day God is going to destroy this world again, not with water but with fire (2 Pet. 3:10-12; see also 2 Thess. 1:7-8). And on that day the angels will say: 'The kingdoms of this world have become the kingdoms of our Lord and of His Christ, and He shall reign forever and ever!' (Rev. 11:15). The only ones who will survive that destruction will be those who have put their trust in Jesus Christ and in His promise to forgive their sins through the atonement of His shed blood. When the apostle John saw 'a great multitude [in heaven] which no one could number' and asked who they were, he was told, 'These are the ones who come out of the great tribulation, and washed their robes and made them white in the blood of the Lamb. Therefore they are before the throne of God and serve Him day and night in His temple' (Rev. 7:9-10,13-15). The power of God at the last judgment will be a terrifying sight. The Bible says that men will cry out 'to the mountains and rocks: "Fall on us and hide us from the face of Him who sits on the throne and from the wrath of the Lamb! For the great day of His wrath has come, and who is able to stand?"' (Rev. 6:14-17). But for those who are trusting in the promise of Christ to cleanse them from all sin through His blood, there need be no fear. God's almighty power will only be used in accord with the promise He has made to us. We can bank on it. God will not break His covenant. He will save the righteous and destroy the wicked.

As with all the other attributes of God, His omnipotence is a great source of inspiration to a Christian in his or her spiritual life. Being one of His many perfections, it is another stimulant to adore a God who is almighty. 'The wondrous and infinite perfections of such a Being,' says Pink, 'call for fervent worship. If men of might and renown claim the admiration of the world, how much more should the power of the Almighty fill us with wonderment and homage. "Who is like unto Thee, O Lord, among the gods, who is like Thee, glorious in holiness, fearful in praises, doing wonders?" (Exod. 15:11)'[3] Praise, too, should be given for the fact that all physical, political and spiritual power in the world today comes from God and is controlled by Him. Violent men, corrupt governments, wily demons can do their utmost, but in the end, by God's all-controlling power, they only succeed in fulfilling God's great plan to overthrow evil and restore paradise. Thus Daniel 4:35 states, 'All the inhabitants of the earth are reputed as nothing; He does according to His will in the army of heaven and among the inhabitants of the earth. No one can restrain His hand or say to Him, "What have You done?"'

There are so many encouragements to be derived from the doctrine of God's omnipotence, but one more will suffice; namely, our Christian service. This is surely the message of Isaiah 40:29-31, 'He gives power to the weak, and to those who have no might He increases

---

3. A.W. Pink, *The Attributes of God*, p. 51.

strength. Even the youths shall faint and be weary, and the young men shall utterly fall, but those who wait on the LORD shall renew their strength; they shall mount up with wings like eagles, they shall run and not be weary, they shall walk and not faint.' Witnessing for Christ in an anti-Christ world is difficult and often discouraging, yet Paul says, 'Let us not grow weary while doing good' (Gal. 6:9). What is the antidote? The answer God gave Paul is in 2 Corinthians 12:9-10, 'And He said to me, "My grace is sufficient for you, for My strength is made perfect in weakness." Therefore most gladly I will rather boast in my infirmities, that the power of Christ may rest upon me. Therefore I take pleasure in infirmities, in reproaches, in needs, in persecutions, in distresses, for Christ's sake. For when I am weak, then I am strong.' Spurgeon elaborates on the answer in this way: 'And now as to thy service, to which thou art called by the Lord. If he be so strong, do not think of thine own weakness any longer, except as being a platform for his strength. Hast thou only one talent? God's Holy Spirit is not limited in power. He can make thine one talent as fruitful as another man's ten. Art thou weak as water? Then rejoice this day, and glory in infirmity, because the power of God shall rest upon thee. Think not of what thou canst do – that is a very small affair, but consider what he can do by thee. He can strengthen the feeble against the strong.'[4]

---

4. C.H. Spurgeon, *The Attributes of God*, (MacDonald, n.d.), p. 23.

7

THE PROVIDENCE OF GOD

In treating God's providence separately, we are distinguishing it from His omnipotence. In essence, however, they belong together. That is why A.W. Pink included God's providence among the attributes of God listed in his book on the subject. Just as God's wisdom is an aspect of God's omniscience, so God's providence is an aspect of God's omnipotence. God's providence has to do with His relation to the world He created. Just as God created the heavens and the earth by His almighty, omnipotent power, so He sustains and governs everything in creation for the glory of His name and the good of His people. They are one and the same power performing different divine functions. By His providence God involves Himself in all events, and directs all things to their foreordained end. Accordingly, The Heidelberg Catechism defines providence as 'the almighty and ever-present power of God whereby He still upholds, as it were by His own hand, heaven and earth together with all creatures, and rules in such a way that leaves and grass, rain and drought, fruitful and unfruitful years, food and drink, health and sickness, riches and poverty, and everything else, come to us not by chance, but by His fatherly hand.' J.I. Packer says, 'The model is of purposive personal management with total "hands-on" control: God is completely in charge of His world. His hand may be hidden, but His rule is absolute.'[1]

Louis Berkhof breaks down the extent of divine providence even further:

> The Bible clearly teaches God's providential control (1) over the universe at large, Ps. 103:19; Dan. 4:35; Eph. 1:11; (2) over the physical world, Job 37:5,10; Ps. 104:14; 135:6; Matt. 5:45; (3) over the brute creation, Ps. 104:21,28; Matt. 6:26; 10:29; (4) over the affairs of nations, Job 12:23; Ps. 22:28; 66:7; Acts 17:26; (5) over man's birth and lot in life, 1 Sam. 16:1; Ps. 139:16; Isa. 45:5; Gal. 1:15,16; (6) over the outward successes and failures of men's lives, Ps. 75:6,7; Luke 1:52; (7) over things seemingly accidental or insignificant, Prov. 16:33; Matt. 10:30; (8) in the protection of the righteous, Ps. 4:8; 5:12; 63:8; 121:3; Rom. 8:28; (9) in supplying the wants of God's people, Gen. 22:8,14; Deut. 8:3; Phil. 4:19; (10) in giving answers to prayer, 1 Sam. 1:19; Isa. 20:5,6; 2 Chron. 33:13; Ps. 65:2; Matt 7:7; Luke 18:7,8; and (11) in the exposure and punishment of the wicked, Ps. 7:12,13, 11:6.[2]

The doctrine of providence teaches us that the world is not ruled by blind forces like chance or fate, but by the omnipotent God who is working out His eternal plan for creation through His only begotten Son, Jesus Christ. For the incarnation of God's Son resulting in His atoning death on the cross and victorious resurrection on the third day are at the centre of all His plans for humankind. Moreover, because God is almighty, He is absolutely sovereign, His dominion is total. He wills as

---

1. J.I. Packer, *Concise Theology* (Tyndale House, 1993), p. 54.

2. L. Berkhof, Systematic Theology, p. 168.

He chooses and carries out all that He wills, for none can stay His hand or thwart His plans. Thus the phrase 'the Lord reigns' or 'God reigns' occurs eight times in Scripture. Psalms 93, 97 and 99 open with the words, 'The LORD reigns.' And right at the end of the Bible God's people in heaven praise Him saying, 'Alleluia! For the Lord God Omnipotent reigns!' (Rev. 19:6; see also Ps. 47:8; 96:10; 1 Chron. 16:31; Isa. 52:7).

In Scripture the picture we are given is of a God who shares His throne with no one else. Thus when Isaiah saw a vision of God in the temple, he says, 'I saw the LORD sitting on a throne' (Isa. 6:1). Again, when Ezekiel was given a vision of God in heaven, he saw 'a throne in appearance like a sapphire stone' and says, 'This was the appearance of the likeness of the glory of the LORD' (Ezek. 1:26-28). Likewise in Revelation chapter 4 a door in heaven is opened and John says, 'Behold, a throne, and One sat on the throne ... who lives forever and ever' (vv. 1-11). The one true, living God of the Bible exercises His power in the world unilaterally. There is no office in heaven where God has to consult with a Cabinet before He makes His decisions. Indeed God's plans were made long before He created anything, even the angels. He is a God of irresistible sovereignty. He wills what He performs, and performs what He wills. Here are some verses to affirm this:

> O LORD God of our fathers, are You not God in heaven, and do You not rule over all the kingdoms of the nations, and in Your hand is there not power and might, so that no one is able to withstand You? (2 Chron. 20:6).

> Then Job answered the LORD and said: 'I know that You can do everything, and that no purpose of Yours can be withheld from You' (Job 42:1-2).

Our God is in heaven: He does whatever He pleases (Ps. 115:3).

The LORD of hosts has sworn, saying, 'Surely, as I have thought, so it shall come to pass, and as I have purposed, so it shall stand' (Isa. 14:24).

'I am God ... and there is no one who can deliver out of My hand; I work, and who will reverse it?' (Isa. 43:12-13).

I am God, and there is no other; I am God, and there is none like Me, declaring the end from the beginning, and from ancient times things that are not yet done, saying, 'My counsel shall stand, and I will do all My pleasure ... Indeed I have spoken it; I will also bring it to pass. I have purposed it; I will also do it' (Isa. 46:9-11).

These Scriptures are more than enough to show that the god of the average person today no more resembles the God of the Bible than the light of a candle resembles the brightness of the sun.

As helpful as these biblical texts are, what is even more helpful is to see the providence of God at work in the lives of His people recorded in the Bible. There are many to choose from, but we shall focus mainly on the life of Joseph in Genesis 37-50.

FAITH SEES THE HIDDEN HAND OF GOD IN PROVIDENCE

Jacob (Abraham's grandson) had twelve sons, and the two youngest, Joseph and Benjamin, were his favourites, because they were the sons of Rachel, his favourite wife (37:3). This turned the ten older brothers against Joseph who was Jacob's particular favourite. Nor did it help matters when Joseph could not refrain from sharing with his brothers his two dreams of rising to greatness with his brothers bowing down to him

(37:5-11). So when Joseph was about seventeen years old, they took advantage of an opportunity to murder him. The ten were feeding their father's flocks a long way from home when Jacob sent Joseph to see how they were doing. But in the providence of God, instead of killing Joseph, they decided it would be more profitable if they sold him to some Midianite traders who were passing by. In the providence of God, when these traders got to Egypt they sold Joseph to Potiphar, 'an officer of Pharaoh'. The brothers, however, did not see God's hand in their evil deed. To them it was just a stroke of luck that the Midianites passed by and took Joseph off their hands, which is what they wanted.

Thirteen years went by, and God was still working out His plan for Joseph and Jacob's family. Potiphar's wife sought to seduce Joseph, but he would have none of it. Enraged, she accused Joseph of assaulting her, and he was unfairly put into prison. There he interpreted favourably a dream of Pharaoh's butler, a fellow-prisoner, who was released shortly afterwards (40:9-14). Then Pharaoh had a dream that none of his wise men could interpret, and the butler, who was now back in Pharaoh's favour, told his master of Joseph's ability to interpret dreams. In Pharaoh's dream, Joseph explained to him that seven years of bumper harvests were going to be followed by seven years of famine. Pharaoh was so impressed, that he appointed Joseph as his Prime Minister to prepare for the coming widespread famine.

Now back in Canaan, when Jacob began to feel the effects of the famine, he sent the ten brothers to buy grain in Egypt, and when they appeared before Joseph he recognized them and decided to test them. He accused them of being spies. And to prove they were not, he took Simeon as a hostage and told them to bring Benjamin back to confirm the story they had told him about their father and his youngest son in Canaan. The brothers, of course, did not know that the stranger was Joseph. They could have supposed he was in Midian. Jacob also, who had been told that Joseph had been killed by a wild beast, could not see God's hand in this either. He balked at Benjamin having to go to Egypt. He said to his sons, 'You have bereaved me of my children: Joseph is no more, Simeon is no more, and you want to take Benjamin away. All these things are against me' (42:36). Actually, they were *for* him, but Jacob and his sons did not have the faith to see it. Joseph, on the other hand, did. Through all his challenging trials, he held on to God, fleeing immorality, and trusting God with his interpretation of dreams. Now with his promotion to high office, Joseph knew that God had sent him to Egypt to save them from the famine. But before he was prepared to care for his brothers, he wanted to be sure that they had learned their lesson and repented of their sin.

The same events were interpreted differently. Jacob and his sons could see nothing but cruel misfortune. Joseph by faith, however, clearly saw God's salvation in it all. And so when he made himself known to his brothers, he said, 'God sent me before you [into Egypt] to preserve a posterity for you in the earth, and to save your lives by a great deliverance' (45:7). That is the key! The things they had not seen which were working out for their good and that of their posterity, all these things, said Joseph, were the doing of God. 'God sent me.' The key to understanding God's providence is faith: the faith of Romans 8:28 which says, 'We know that all things work together for good to those who love God, to those who are the called according to His purpose.' Unless we believe in the hidden hand of God in providence, the events of life are meaningless.

ALL NATURAL EVENTS ARE GOVERNED BY GOD'S WILL

The seven years of famine in Joseph's day were sent by the God who creates and sustains. Nothing happens in the world that is not predetermined by God 'who upholds all things through the word of His power' (Heb. 1:3). God's hand was in the lightning that destroyed all Job's sheep and in the wind that struck the house where Job's children were having a party, killing them all. For when Job learned of these events 'he fell to the ground and worshipped. And he said, "Naked I came from my mother's womb, and naked I shall return there. The LORD gave, and the LORD has taken away; blessed be the name of the LORD." In all this Job did not sin nor charge God with wrong' (Job 1:20-22). Again, when God was punishing Israel for their sins, He says in Amos 4:7, 'I also withheld rain from you, when there were still three months to the harvest. I made it rain on one city; I withheld rain from another city.'

Day by day, the God who created the world governs everything in it even to the smallest detail as our Lord so delightfully puts it: 'Are not two sparrows sold for a copper coin? And not one of them falls to the ground apart from your Father's will. But the very hairs of your head are all numbered. Do not fear therefore; you are of more value than many sparrows' (Matt. 10:29-31). In other words, God's care of us extends to the loss of our hair! He knows their number, because not one is lost apart from His will. That is the extent of God's rule over all natural events, great and small.

GOD'S PROVIDENCE IS PARTICULAR IN HIS CONTROL OF HUMAN AFFAIRS

'God sent me' (Gen. 45:7). In saying that, Joseph was not claiming some sort of unique importance. Not in the least. He was simply acknowledging a truth that is found everywhere in the Bible: that God directs and uses every event in every person's life to accomplish its divinely appointed end. Thus we read in Scripture:

> Whatever the LORD pleases, He does, in heaven and in earth, in the seas and in all deep places (Psalm 135:6).

> A man's heart plans his way, but the LORD directs his steps ... the lot is cast into the lap, but its every decision is from the LORD (Prov. 16:9,33).

> There are many plans in a man's heart, nevertheless the LORD's counsel — that will stand (Prov. 19:21).

> The king's heart is in the hand of the LORD, like the rivers of water; He turns it wherever He wishes (Prov. 21:1).

> O LORD, I know the way of man is not in himself; it is not in man who walks to direct his own steps (Jer. 10:23).

> 'O house of Israel, can I not do with you as this potter?' says the LORD. 'Look, as the clay is in the potter's hand, so are you in My hand, O house of Israel!' (Jer. 18:6).

> In Him also we have obtained an inheritance, being predestined according to the purpose of Him who works all things according to the counsel of His will (Eph. 1:11).

Of course, we choose what we want to do and when to do it; but behind our freedom to choose is the sovereignty of God that overrules and sees that His will is always accomplished in whatever we do. God in His providence directs the affairs of all men and women in the world, both the powerful and the ordinary people, and the story that highlights this in a wonderful way is an event in King Ahab's life. In 2 Chronicles 18 we read how the king of Israel went into battle against the Syrians disguised as an ordinary soldier in order to avoid being killed. For 'the king of Syria had commanded the captains of the chariots who were with him, saying, "Fight with no one small or great, but only with the king of Israel."' But Ahab, who was one of Israel's most wicked kings, did not allow for the providence of God over the affairs of men. So we read, 'Now a certain man drew a bow at random and struck the king of Israel between the joints of his armour ... and about the time of sunset he died' (vv. 30-34). And the dogs licked his blood as God predicted. That is amazing! A great king dies by the hand of an enemy archer who shoots his bow 'at random'. He did not aim at anything specifically, but God's will was done. How God makes His will in the affairs of men come to pass without violating human free agency, is a mystery to us. 'His hand may be hidden, but His rule is absolute' (J.I. Packer).

GOD'S PROVIDENTIAL RULE INCLUDES MAN'S EVIL DEEDS

In Genesis 45:4-8 we read, 'Then he said: "I am Joseph your brother, whom you sold into Egypt. But now, do not be grieved nor angry with yourselves because you sold me here; for God sent me before you to preserve life ... to preserve a posterity for you in the earth and to save your lives by a great deliverance. So now it was not you who sent me here, but God."' However, in pointing this out, Joseph was not excusing or covering up the wickedness of his brothers' hatred that made them sell him into slavery. Not at all! For Joseph goes on to say in chapter 50:20, 'But as for you, you meant evil against me; but God meant it for good in order to bring it about as it is this day, to save many people alive.' Now that is an incredible thing! It is not a case of two opposite wills in conflict with each other, and the will of God changing man's will. Rather, it is an amazing picture of God's holy will being carried out without in any way interfering with man's will or being a partaker in or condoner of his evil. Of course, we cannot explain how that can be possible, but it is true. It is something that belongs to the inscrutable omniscience and omnipotence of God. The Bible clearly says that God condemns evil and punishes it. When Joseph's brothers sold him into slavery, God hated their sin. For thirteen years they had to live with their aged father's grief.

In Romans 9 Paul uses another incident in Egypt to illustrate this same point. It involved the Pharaoh who lived nearly 400 years after Joseph and would not let Israel return to Canaan. Looking at how God's will is done, Paul asks the question: 'Is there unrighteousness with God? Certainly not! For He says to Moses: "I will have mercy on whomever I will have mercy, and I will have compassion on whomever I will have compassion." So then it is not of him who wills, nor of him who runs, but of God who shows mercy. For the Scripture says to Pharaoh, "Even for this same purpose I have raised you up, that I may show My power in you, and that My name may be declared in all the earth"' (vv. 14-17). What is Paul referring to? He is referring to the fact that when Pharaoh wilfully hardened his heart and would not give God's people their freedom, he too was unwittingly accomplishing God's will. 'Therefore', says Paul, 'He has mercy on whom He wills, and whom He wills He hardens. You will say to me then, "Why does He still find fault? For who has resisted His will?"' And Paul's answer is: 'O man, who are you to reply against God?' (vv. 18-20). When Pharaoh hardened his heart, it was his doing and not God's. The fact that God used Pharaoh's hardness of heart to show His power in the miraculous plagues that were brought upon Egypt, did not condone Pharaoh's evil, or exonerate him. To quote Matthew Henry, 'What is corrupt, though of God's permitting, is not of His planting.'[3]

But the supreme example of God's providential rule over the evil deeds of men is the crucifixion of God's Son on Calvary. How did it come about? It came about through the malice of the Jewish priests and the injustice of Pontius Pilate. It was their evil intent that the loving and holy Son of God who posed a threat to their positions, should be put to death. Peter, however, says in Acts 2:23, 'Jesus of Nazareth ... being delivered by the determined counsel and foreknowledge of God, you have taken by lawless hands, have crucified, and put to death.' What Pilate and the Jews did in putting Jesus to death was a violation of the law of God and of men. It was judicial murder. That is what they wanted and that is what they did. But in carrying out their evil deed, they did not thwart God's will for His Son. On the contrary, Peter says in Acts 4:27-28, 'For truly against Your holy Servant Jesus, whom You anointed, both Herod and Pontius Pilate, with the Gentiles and the people of Israel, were gathered together to do whatever Your hand and Your purpose determined before to be done.' That is the glorious truth of God's overruling providence. Without inciting or interfering in the evil actions of men, God perfectly accomplishes His eternal purposes in the world through them.

MAN'S SALVATION IS THE APPOINTED END OF GOD'S PROVIDENCE

Thus Joseph says, 'God sent me before you to preserve a posterity for you in the earth, and to save your lives

---

3. Matthew Henry, quoted by John Blanchard, *More Gathered Gold* (Evangelical Press, 1986), p. 256.

by a great deliverance' (Gen. 45:7). The doctrine of providence teaches Christians that their destiny is not determined by blind forces such as chance or fate. They are not even at the mercy of the devil, for the devil cannot do anything without first getting permission from God to do so. God permits or 'allows' evil without ever authorising it (Acts 14:16; James 1:13). This is plainly taught in the book of Job. Before Satan could harm a hair on Job's head, he had to get permission from God (Job 1:6-12). The devil is God's devil, Luther used to say. Like all the other angels, God created him sinless and perfect to love and serve his Creator, but that was not good enough for Satan. In his pride he wanted to be worshipped rather than being a worshipper, and so he led a rebellion against God and took one third of the angels with him (Rev. 12:4,9).

God could have destroyed these adversaries immediately, but in His wisdom and sovereignty He allowed them some limited freedom. Indeed the Bible says that Satan is bound by 'a great chain' (Rev. 20:1), so his activities are restricted by God. Every evil plot he hatches, only turns out to God's advantage. For God remains on His throne exercising 'total hands-on control'. Nothing can or does happen that is not used to achieve His appointed end, which is to save a special people out of all the nations for His glory and their good (Deut. 7:6; Eph. 1:3-6; Rev. 7:9-17). If we want no part of that purpose, the doctrine of God's providence will be of no comfort to us. Only Christians can have the assurance that all that happens to them is divinely planned, and that each event is a fresh call to rejoice in the knowledge that it is all working out for our good (Rom. 8:28); for our own personal sanctification in this life and our glorification in the hereafter (Dan. 12:1-3; 2 Thess. 1:10; 1 John 3:1-3).

Those who try to resist God's will and sovereign rule are fighting a losing battle. They may gain a few riches and pleasures now, but they will lose their soul in the end (Matt. 16:24-26). Let us put our faith in Jesus Christ today and become one of 'the called according to His purpose' and find forgiveness and rest for our soul in the care of God's sovereign grace.

> My life is but a weaving between my God and me.
> I do not choose the colours, He worketh steadily.
> Ofttimes He weaveth sorrow, and I in foolish pride
> Forget He sees the upper, and I the under side.
> Not till the loom is silent and the shuttles cease to fly
> Will God unroll the canvas and explain the
>   reason why
> The dark threads are as needful in the skilful
>   Weaver's hand
> As the threads of gold and silver, in the pattern
>   He has planned.
>
>   *(Anonymous)*

8

THE IMMUTABILITY OF GOD

What do theologians mean by the term *the immutability of God?* The adjective *mutable* describes something liable to change or alteration resulting in it becoming different. Immutable, therefore, is the opposite. It describes something unchangeable; not liable to alteration or variation in form, nature, or substance. The doctrine of the immutability of God, then, admits of no change in God in respect to what He has revealed of Himself in His holy, infallible word, the Bible. To be more precise, God is unchangeable in respect to His (1) essence (God can neither gain nor lose any attributes of deity); (2) character (God can become neither better nor worse morally); (3) veracity (God's word cannot be true sometimes and false at other times); (4) purpose (God's decrees are unalterable). This is the basic outline that the great Christian writers of the past and the present have followed: Thomas Watson (1620-1686), Stephen Charnock (1628-1680), C.H. Spurgeon (1834-1892), A.W. Pink (1886-1952), J.I. Packer (1926-), and we will follow suit.

Now is it really important to be certain that God is immutable? Is this attribute as important as the attributes of God's being that we have considered so far? Indeed it is! For as the omnipresence, omniscience and omnipotence of God are essential to His deity, so He could not be God without being immutable or unchangeably divine. If God were subject to change, then He could become less powerful, less knowledgeable and no longer everywhere present. The immutability of God is also very important to us personally, because we live in a world of change. The sun rises and sets, the moon waxes and wanes, the seasons come and go, we enter into the world and then leave it again. We need a solid rock to give us stability in the ebb and flow of life; 'You keep him in perfect peace whose mind is stayed on you, because he trusts in you. Trust in the LORD forever, because the LORD GOD is an everlasting rock' (Isa. 26:3-4, ESV). We could have no secure and meaningful relationship to God like believers in Bible times had, if He were subject to change. We are thrilled at all God did for them, but how can we be sure that He is willing and able to do the same for us? J.I. Packer's answer is:

> The sense of remoteness is an illusion which springs from seeking the link between our situation and that of the various Bible characters in the wrong place. It is true that in terms of space, time, and culture, they, and the historic epoch to which they belonged, are a very long way away from us. But the link between them and us is not found at that level. The link is God Himself. For the God with whom they had to do is the same God with whom we have to do. We could sharpen the point by saying, *exactly* the same God; for God does not change in the least particular.[1]

---

1. J.I. Packer, Knowing God, p. 68.

GOD'S *BEING* CANNOT CHANGE

By God's being we mean the properties which belong to the divine essence in the sense that He cannot add any attribute to those which He has always had, nor lose any which He already has. In either case it would mean that God was incomplete or imperfect and therefore not divine. So God is, necessarily, incapable of change. He is an eternal, infinite and perfect Spirit whose attributes will remain what they have always been. He cannot grow older, or wiser, or stronger, or holier. In Exodus 3:14 God revealed His name to Moses as 'I am who I am', which was a declaration of His self-existence and His eternal changelessness. He has no beginning or ending. This claim is repeated, in one way or another, many times in Scripture. For example:

Before the mountains were brought forth, or ever You had formed the earth and the world, even from everlasting to everlasting, You are God (Ps. 90:2).

Of old You founded the earth, and the heavens are the work of Your hands. Even they will perish, but You endure; and all of them will wear out like a garment; like clothing You will change them and they will be changed. But You are the same, and Your years will not come to an end (Ps. 102:25-27).

Before Me there was no God formed, and there will be none after Me (Isa. 43:10).

For I am the LORD, I do not change; therefore you, O sons of Jacob, are not consumed (Mal. 3:6).

He who is the blessed and only Potentate, the King of kings and Lord of lords, who alone has immortality, dwelling in unapproachable light, whom no man has seen or can see, to whom be honor and everlasting power. Amen (1 Tim. 6:15-16).

Jesus Christ is the same yesterday, today, and forever (Heb. 13:8).

Now if God is immutable in His being, how do we explain the miracle of the incarnation when 'the Word [who] was God ... became flesh and dwelt among us ... full of grace and truth' (John 1:1,14), when 'God was manifested in the flesh' (1 Tim. 3:16)? Did the being of the second person of the Trinity change from what it always was when the Word became flesh? In trying to answer that question we must always remember that the difficult revelations of truth in Scripture must always be understood and interpreted in the light of the clear and simple statements. With that in mind, we can say that the divine being can never alter in any way. To quote Tozer, 'When Jesus was born of the virgin Mary, He took a tabernacle on Himself, but His deity didn't become humanity ... That which is not God cannot become God. And that which is God cannot become that which is not God.'[2] How then did the early Christian Church resolve the issue? The Council of Chalcedon (A.D. 451) affirmed that Jesus is one divine-human person in two natures, and that the two natures are united in His personal being without mixture, confusion, separation, or division; and that each nature retained its own attributes. How this can be so is an unsolvable mystery for finite creatures.

The great difference, then, between the Creator and His creatures is that their being is subject to change and His is not. He is eternally the same. His glory never fades. So it is not surprising that *Abide with me* was a favourite funeral hymn of former generations:

Swift to its close ebbs out life's little day;
Earth's joys grow dim, its glories pass away;

2.   A.W. Tozer, *The Attributes of God*, vol. 2, p. 97.

Change and decay in all around I see:
O Thou who changest not, abide with me.

Hold Thou Thy cross before my closing eyes,
Shine through the gloom, and point me to the skies;
Heaven's morning breaks, and earth's vain
   shadows flee;
In life, in death, O Lord, abide with me.

          (H. F. Lyte, 1793-1847)

GOD'S *CHARACTER* CANNOT CHANGE

Unlike their Creator, the character of His creatures can change according to their circumstances. We are fallen creatures due to Adam and Eve's disobedience, and as a result we can sometimes be honest and well-behaved, at other times dishonest and misbehave. Stress caused by war, or famine, or abuse, or addiction (to name just a few circumstances) can also alter a person's conduct for the worse. The same can be said of old age and mental disorders. But our Creator is not liable to any changes of character. God is absolutely, unalterably, morally perfect. He is totally free of sin and completely full of goodness in the sense of holiness, love, mercy, generosity, faithfulness, and justice (or righteousness). To quote C.S. Storms, 'If God could change (or become) in respect to His moral character, it would be either for the better or the worse. If for the better, it would indicate that He had been morally imperfect or incomplete antecedent to the time of change, and hence never God. If for the worse, it would indicate that He is now morally less perfect or complete, i.e. subsequent to the time of change, and hence no longer God.'[3]

God's perfect character is today what it always was and what it always will be. In Exodus 34:6-8 we have a list of virtues that describe the perfect

---

3. C.S. Storms, *The Grandeur of God*, pp. 110-111.

135

character of God: 'And the LORD passed before him [Moses] and proclaimed, "The LORD, the LORD God, merciful and gracious, longsuffering, and abounding in goodness and truth, keeping mercy for thousands, forgiving iniquity and transgression and sin, by no means clearing the guilty, visiting the iniquity of the fathers upon the children and the children's children to the third and the fourth generation." So Moses made haste and bowed his head toward the earth, and worshiped.' God's moral character is perfect and changeless, worthy of the highest eternal praise of His people. No wonder the psalmist cries out: 'Oh, taste and see that the LORD is good; blessed is the man who trusts in Him! Oh, fear the LORD, you His saints! There is no want to those who fear Him. The young lions lack and suffer hunger; but those who seek the LORD shall not lack any good thing' (Ps. 34:8-10; see also 1 Pet. 2:3).

How blessed believers are to be the beneficiaries of God's infinite goodness which never varies, as James so vividly describes: 'Every good gift and every perfect gift is from above, and comes down from the Father of lights, with whom there is no variation or shadow of turning' (1:17). The sun never stays in the same place from our observation, and so the shadow it casts varies as it moves. God's character, however, never varies. He remains forever the God who is both gracious and just. He forgives and saves those who put their trust in Him, and condemns and punishes those who rebel against Him.

GOD'S *WORD* CANNOT CHANGE

It is common today to hear politicians or other prominent people retract a previous statement by simply saying, 'I misspoke.' The man in the street often has to change his story because the facts do not back him up. Sometimes we have to correct previous statements because our opinions have changed. Other times we do not stand by the truth because it is inconvenient. Even the laws of our land are constantly subject to change. We cannot depend on the words of human beings. More often than not they will prove unreliable. God's spoken words recorded in Scripture, however, are totally dependable and inerrant. God Himself is 'truth'. Thus our Lord Jesus Christ, 'God manifested in the flesh', said, 'I am ... the truth' (John 14:6); 'Your word is truth' (John 17:17); and 'the Scripture cannot be broken' (John 10:35). Nothing can cancel or invalidate God's word. His promises cannot be voided, His warnings cannot be dismissed, His pronouncements cannot be disputed, and His predictions cannot fail to come to pass.

Thus the psalmist says, 'Forever, O LORD, Your word is settled [literally, stands firm] in heaven' (Ps. 119:89). In Isaiah 40:6-8 we read: '... All flesh is grass, and all its loveliness is like the flower of the field. The grass withers, the flower fades, because the breath of the LORD blows upon it; surely the people are grass. The grass withers, the flower fades, but the word of our God stands forever.' Our Lord Jesus closes His Olivet discourse by giving us this assurance: 'Heaven and earth will pass away, but My words will by no means pass away' (Matt. 24:35). There would be less uncertainty and fear if Christians would only hold on to this great truth. God's word will stand firm against all its deniers. It will prevail over all its enemies. It will be fully vindicated in every instance, because it is truth unchanged and unchanging. To quote our Lord again, 'For assuredly, I say to you, till heaven and earth pass away, one jot [the smallest letter in the Hebrew alphabet] or one tittle [ornamental curl of Hebrew letters] will by no means pass from the law [general term for God's word] till all is fulfilled' (Matt. 5:18; see also Luke 16:17).

GOD'S *PRINCIPLES OF JUDGMENT*
CANNOT CHANGE

God is absolutely consistent in the way He treats all people. In 1 Peter 1:17 the apostle speaks of God as 'the Father, who without partiality judges according to each one's work'. Paul emphasises the same principle in Romans 2:5-11. He speaks of 'the righteous judgment of God, who "will render to each one according to his deeds": eternal life to those who by patient continuance in doing good seek for glory, honour, and immortality; but to those who are self-seeking and do not obey the truth, but obey unrighteousness – indignation and wrath, tribulation and anguish, on every soul of man who does evil, of the Jew first and also of the Greek; but glory, honour, and peace to everyone who works what is good, to the Jew first and also to the Greek. For there is no partiality with God.' All men and women are spiritual rebels who oppose God, and it is only 'the goodness of God that leads you to repentance', says Paul in the same chapter, verse 4.

Those who by God's grace turn from their sin and seek His mercy, obtain the forgiveness of their sins and eternal life through the atoning death of His Son, Jesus Christ (Matt. 26:28; John 3:14-18). But those who persistently turn a deaf ear to God's convicting voice through conscience and Scripture, will die in their sins and suffer eternal torment (Matt. 13:41-42; John 3:36). That is how we find God dealing with people throughout the pages of the Bible, and that is how He deals with us still. Men and women may change in their attitude and actions towards us. It is one of the sad facts of life. A person can be your friend one day, and then because of some perceived or imagined slight have nothing more to do with you. They have changed their assessment of you for no apparent reason. But the principles governing God's dealings with human beings are constant. He never acts unpredictably or indiscriminately, but always justly.

There are, however, several passages in Scripture which speak of God not carrying out His intention to punish people for egregiously sinning against Him. One thinks of God's stated intention to destroy the nation of Israel (Exod. 32:9-14), or to end the life of King Hezekiah (Isa. 38:1-6), or to destroy the city of Nineveh, to name a few examples. Louis Berkhof is helpful here in pointing out that, 'if Scripture speaks of His repenting, changing His intention, and altering His relation to sinners when they repent, we should remember that this is only an anthropopathic [human] way of speaking. In reality the change is not in God, but in man and in man's relations to God.'[4]

The instances cited above should all be understood as true expressions of God's present intention of dealing with each situation as it existed at that particular time. His justice demanded judgment. But when Moses and Hezekiah prayed and asked for mercy, God acted consistently with His divine nature to be merciful and forgiving. Israel was spared and Hezekiah's life was extended for another fifteen years. God is true to all His attributes all the time. The example of Jonah preaching to Nineveh is even more explicit (Jonah 3:1-10). God sent the prophet to this 'exceedingly great city' to warn them, saying, 'Yet forty days and Nineveh shall be overthrown ... So the people of Nineveh

---

4. Louis Berkhof, *Systematic Theology*, p. 59.

believed God, proclaimed a fast, and put on sackcloth, from the greatest to the least of them.' The purpose for proclaiming a divine warning is to lead people to repentance. So because the repentance of the people of Nineveh was genuine, we read, 'Then God saw their works, that they turned from their evil way, and God relented from the disaster that He had said He would bring upon them, and He did not do it.'

Once the people repented, the situation was different, and God responded differently to that changed situation. What God did was not a violation of His immutability. On the contrary, had God gone ahead and destroyed the people of Nineveh in spite of their being repentant, it would have shown Him to be changeable and not dependable. It would have shown Him to be a God who sometimes is pleased with a penitent spirit and at other times is not. That is not the God of the Bible. True, there was a change in God's attitude to these evil people when they repented, but not a change in the way He always deals with sinful beings. It is a principle of God's righteous immutable being that He consistently punishes the impenitent, while consistently forgiving the penitent.

GOD'S *DECREES* CANNOT CHANGE

The word *decree* (sometimes translated 'counsel') occurs again and again in the Bible, and simply refers to God's eternal plan to have for Himself a redeemed people for His glory; a plan for the 'Seed' of the 'woman' to 'bruise' the serpent's 'head' and bring salvation to all Adam's fallen race who look to Him for it (Gen. 3:15). The Westminster Shorter Catechism provides this classic definition: 'The decrees of God are His eternal purpose, according to the counsel of His will, whereby, for His own glory, He has fore-ordained whatever comes to pass.' The decree of God, then, is His eternal, all-embracing, unchangeable, and efficacious purpose to save a people for Himself which no one can number (Rev. 7:9-10). Here are some references to God's decree:

> I will declare the decree: the LORD has said to Me, 'You are My Son, today I have begotten You. Ask of Me, and I will give You the nations for Your inheritance, and the ends of the earth for Your possession. You shall break them with a rod of iron; You shall dash them to pieces like a potter's vessel' (Ps. 2:7-9).

> The LORD brings the counsel of the nations to nothing; He makes the plans of the peoples of no effect. The counsel of the LORD stands forever, the plans of His heart to all generations (Ps. 33:10-11).

> The LORD of hosts has sworn, saying, 'Surely as I have thought, so shall it come to pass, and as I have purposed, so it shall stand' (Isa. 14:24).

> In Him also we have obtained an inheritance, being predestined [for that inheritance] according to the purpose of Him who works all things according to the counsel of His will (Eph. 1:11).

That is what God has decreed. His Son is going to rule a people gathered out of all nations. And what God has planned in eternity He carries out in time. It is happening before our eyes. God's decrees do not change. All that He purposed in eternity and has committed Himself in Scripture to do, will infallibly be done in His time. God will not change His plan one iota, nor can anyone stop it from happening.

Moreover, because God is sovereign, He accomplishes all His plans using the free and willing activity of men. He does not violate their wills to achieve His appointed ends. Proverbs 19:21 says, 'There are many plans in a man's heart, nevertheless the LORD's counsel

– that will stand.' Men and women have to change their plans, because they lack the ability to foresee obstacles down the road and do not have the resources to overcome them. But God never has to change His plan of action, because He is both omniscient and omnipotent. His plans are made on the basis of His complete knowledge of all the obstacles in the way and His almighty power to overcome them. So when the backslidden prophet Balaam was hired by king Balak to put a curse on Israel, whom God had decreed to bless, he did not succeed. And when the king asked the prophet why he was not able to curse Israel, Balaam replied, 'God is not a man, that He should lie, nor a son of man, that He should repent [or change His mind]. Has He said, and will He not do it? Or has He spoken, and will He not make it good?' (Num. 23:19). No wonder Hebrews 6:17 speaks of 'the immutability of His counsel.' All God's decrees (all His holy, wise and loving purposes) made in eternity past, but now revealed in Scripture, will unfailingly be carried out in time. Not one little detail of His plan will change. In Isaiah 46:9-11 God says, 'For I am God, and there is no other; I am God, and there is none like Me, declaring the end from the beginning, and from ancient times things that are not yet done, saying, "My counsel shall stand, and I will do all My pleasure" … I have purposed it; I will also do it.'

The doctrine of God's immutability can bring great comfort to us if we are true believers in the Lord Jesus Christ. Psalm 146:3 says, 'Do not put your trust in princes, nor in a son of man, in whom there is no help.' Human beings cannot be relied upon, but God can. Has He promised to forgive all our sins if we put our trust in Christ's atoning death to save us from our sins? Has He promised to give us the Holy Spirit to transform us increasingly into Christ's likeness? Has He promised to complete the saving work He has begun in us and bring us at last to glory? God has! (Acts 26:18; John 16:13-14; 2 Cor. 3:18; John 10:27-30). And the immutability of God guarantees that He will. In Isaiah 54:10 He says, 'For the mountains shall depart and the hills be removed, but My kindness shall not depart from you, nor shall My covenant of peace be removed, says the LORD who has mercy on you.' Romans 8:38-39 is even more assuring, 'For I am persuaded that neither death nor life, nor angels nor principalities nor powers, nor things present nor things to come, nor height nor depth nor any other created being, shall be able to separate us from the love of God which is in Christ Jesus our Lord.' Why? Because 'Jesus Christ is the same yesterday, today and forever', and 'therefore He is also able to save to the uttermost those who come to God through Him, since He ever lives to make intercession for them' (Heb. 13:8; 7:25).

On the other hand, if God's immutability is a comfort to all true believers, it is a very discomforting truth for every unbeliever. Those who defy God's will and live as if He did not exist, will find that if they die in unbelief and in their sins, they will go into everlasting punishment. God will not deny Himself by overlooking their sins and tolerating injustice in His world. He is unchangeably holy and just, and must act accordingly. His decree in Psalm 9:17 is, 'The wicked shall be turned into hell, and all the nations that forget God.' The apostle Paul writes of a time 'when the Lord Jesus is revealed from heaven with His mighty angels, in flaming fire taking vengeance on those who do not know God, and on those who do not obey the gospel of our Lord Jesus Christ. These shall be punished with everlasting destruction from the presence of the Lord and from the glory of His power' (2 Thess. 1:7-9).

Every sinner in the Bible who came to God through faith in Christ, His promised Messiah and Saviour, found grace in His eyes to be pardoned and reconciled to God. Take hope, then, in the immutability of God, and trust Him to treat you in the same just, merciful way He has treated all penitent sinners from the beginning of time (Ps. 51:1-4; Luke 18:9-14).

How good is the God we adore!
Our faithful, unchangeable friend:
His love is as great as His pow'r
And knows neither measure nor end.

For Christ is the first and the last;
His Spirit will guide us safe home;
We'll praise Him for all that is past
And trust Him for all that's to come.

(J. Hart, 1712-1768)

PART II:

THE COMMUNICABLE ATTRIBUTES OF GOD'S CHARACTER

9

THE HOLINESS OF GOD

In our study so far we have been considering the attributes of God's *being* or essence; namely, His transcendence, triunity, omnipresence, omniscience, wisdom, omnipotence, providence and immutability. These are attributes that constitute God's *greatness*. God, however, also has attributes of *character* which are essential moral qualities that constitute His *goodness*. These are qualities that concern His holiness, love, grace, faithfulness, jealousy, and wrath in infinite measure, and which He communicates to His people in finite measure.

As we begin with the subject of God's holiness, it will help to be reminded by Packer that 'the word signifies everything about God that sets Him apart from us and makes Him an object of awe, adoration, and dread to us. It covers all aspects of His transcendent greatness and moral perfection and thus is an attribute of all His attributes, pointing to the "Godness" of God at every point. Every facet of God's nature and every aspect of His character may properly be spoken of as holy, just because it is His. The core of the concept, however, is

God's purity, which cannot tolerate any form of sin (Hab. 1:13) and thus calls sinners to constant self-abasement in His presence (Isa. 6:5).'[1]

So in the Bible, God's power is a holy power; His wisdom is a holy wisdom; His sovereignty is a holy rule; His love is a holy love; His wrath is a holy anger; His word is a holy word. God's holiness is the glory and the beauty of all His attributes:

Who is like You, O LORD, among the gods? Who is like You, glorious in holiness? (Exod. 15:11).

Sing praise to the LORD, you saints of His, and give thanks at the remembrance of His holy name (Ps. 30:4).

Exalt the LORD our God, and worship at His footstool – He is holy (Ps. 99:5).

He has sent redemption to His people; He has commanded His covenant forever: holy and awesome is His name (Ps. 111:9).

O LORD my God, my Holy One ... You are of purer eyes than to behold evil, and cannot look on wickedness (Hab. 1:12-13).

This is the message which we have heard from Him and declare to you, that God is light and in Him is no darkness at all (1 John 1:5).

Who shall not fear You, O Lord, and glorify Your name? For You alone are holy (Rev. 15:4).

HOLINESS IS A DIFFICULT CONCEPT

Unlike God's other attributes, we have nothing to compare His holiness with. In addition, as H.R. Macintosh points out, 'The proposal to define God may well appear symptomatic of irreverence. He is the

---

1. J.I. Packer, *Concise Theology*, p. 43.

Infinite One, and to define is in logic to make Him finite, or has a look of that. "Canst thou find out the Almighty unto perfection?" is a warning word from the past.[2] As a result, holiness is one of the most misunderstood words in any language. The average person thinks it is a pompous, 'I am better than you' attitude. Holiness is equated in their eyes with being sanctimonious and making a show of your piety and religious fervour. But nothing could be further from the truth as far as God's holiness is concerned.

The fact is that although holiness is difficult to explain because we have nothing in a fallen world to compare it with, it is nevertheless a concept that we can experience. It is something that men and women sensed or felt in Bible times even though no human being has ever set eyes on the fullness of the Divine Being. When God did appear to various people from time to time, it was always in a veiled form that portrayed only a fraction of the infinite distance and difference that there is between Him and ourselves. Sometimes it was in the form of a man (a theophany), or fire, or cloud, or a voice, or blinding light (Gen. 16:7-13; Exod. 3:2; Judges 6:11-24; 13:2-22; 1 Kings 19:11-15; Matt. 17:5-6; Acts 9:4-6). But in whatever form God did appear to His people, they knew they were in the presence of the Almighty Creator of heaven and earth who is utterly separate from the evil and sin of the world, and they prostrated themselves in worship and awe.

Even when God appeared before them in human form, their response was far more than the mere obeisance they would offer an earthly king. It was something over and above that. They were filled with awe, and with 'the fear of the LORD' (2 Chron. 19:9; Prov. 1:7; Acts 9:31, etc). That is what the Bible means when it calls God

---

2. H.R. Macintosh, *The Christian Apprehension of God*, p. 155.

holy. It signifies everything about God that sets Him apart from all creation (especially His moral perfection and unsullied purity), and which therefore makes Him an object of awe and fear. Psalm 99:1,3 (ESV) captures the experience beautifully. 'The LORD reigns; let the peoples tremble! He sits enthroned upon the cherubim, let the earth quake! ... Let them praise Your great and awesome name! Holy is He!'

It is the same emotion Isaiah experienced in the temple when he saw God who alone is holy (Isa. 6:1-3). All of a sudden there was a manifestation of God's presence 'sitting on a throne, high and lifted up, and the train of His robe filled the temple. Above it stood seraphim; each one had six wings: with two he covered his face [because the holiness of God was too bright to gaze upon], with two he covered his feet [in modesty, because though he was sinless, he was still only a creature] and with two he flew [for angels are messengers as well as ministering spirits]. And one cried to another and said: "Holy, holy, holy is the LORD of hosts; the whole earth is full of His glory!"' When a word is repeated three times like that in Hebrew, it is a bit like in mathematics when you raised a number to a higher power, 'Holy, holy, holy' is holiness cubed. 'A cube', says Charnock, is 'a piece of metal or wood framed four square; when every side is exactly of the same equality, cast it which way you will, it will always be in the same posture, because it is equal to itself in all its dimensions.'[3]

No wonder Isaiah goes on to say, 'And the posts of the door were shaken by the voice of him who cried out, and the house was filled with smoke. So I said: "Woe is me, for I am undone! Because I am a man of unclean lips, and I dwell in the midst of a people of

---

3. Stephen Charnock, *The Existence and Attributes of God*, p. 104.

unclean lips; for my eyes have seen the King, the LORD of hosts"' (vv. 4-5). Isaiah was overcome with the sight of God's holiness and filled with a sense of awe and fear. That is what God's holiness does to those who are confronted by it. It fills a person with awe and fear. When anyone encountered the God of the Bible, that is what they experienced: some more than others, depending on how great their exposure to God's holiness was.

GOD IN HIS BEING IS TOTALLY SEPARATE FROM EVERYTHING

It is important to understand that one of the great tasks of the Old Testament was to instil awe and fear when people worshipped God, while at the same time teaching them that God in His grace has made a way for communication and fellowship between Himself and penitent human beings. The rituals and laws governing the way the Jews were to approach God and what happened to those who did not observe them were intended to create awe and fear of God's infinite, almighty and holy Being. As far as we can get any meaning from the origin of the word 'holy', the root idea is 'to cut off' or 'to set apart'. And so in the Old Testament the Hebrew word for holy is the opposite of the word for common or ordinary. In other words, God is utterly separate from the whole secular realm.

Now this was taught in two ways. To begin with, the Old Testament warned the Israelites that it was dangerous to come near this holy God. For example, when Moses was to ascend Mount Sinai to receive the Ten Commandments from God, 'there were thunderings and lightnings, so that all the people trembled' (Exod. 19:16). Moreover, God said (v. 12): 'Whoever touches the mountain shall surely be put to death.' Why? The answer given is: 'that His fear may be before you, so that you may not sin' (Exod. 20:20). Again, when the Philistines captured and then returned to Israel the Ark of the Covenant (the symbol of God's presence) because God had struck their men with 'tumours' for taking it, the Israelites were also punished when they dared to look into the Ark of the Lord. 1 Samuel 6:19 says that over fifty thousand men died 'because the LORD had struck the people with a great slaughter'. As a result, everyone was afraid to carry the Ark back to its proper resting place in Shiloh. It remained in Kirjath Jearim for twenty years until David brought it home.

But even David did not follow the divine procedure for transporting the Ark. He had it transported on an ox wagon, instead of being carried by the priests. He probably thought the twenty-five miles was too far for the priests to carry it on their shoulders. When the oxen stumbled and 'Uzzah put out his hand to the Ark of God and took hold of it ... the anger of the LORD was aroused against Uzzah, and God struck him there for his error, and he died there by the Ark of the LORD' (2 Sam. 6:7). In these ways God was communicating the important truth that it is dangerous to come near this God whose holiness utterly cuts Him off from sinners. Like with fire and straw, unless great precautions are taken, certain destruction will take place when sinners get too near God.

The other way that the Old Testament sought to impart this sense of fear before the holiness and separateness of God was by stressing the need for worshippers to be ceremonially cleansed. For it was only by religious rituals such as washing their clothes and bodies, and by sprinkling the blood of animal sacrifices on the altar of God that the righteous anger of God was contained. Of course, only the priests could enter the temple and offer sacrifices to make communion with this holy God possible. But they had to meticulously follow the regulations that God had laid down if they were to be preserved from the danger of perishing before His awful holiness. The ordinary people could have no access to God, only the priests who were their appointed mediators with God.

In this way, the people of Israel got the message loud and clear that God is wholly separate from sinners and only approachable through the death of an innocent substitute. It was designed to instil awe and fear before the holiness of God and it did so by stressing the transcendent greatness of God's being. He is not our "chum". He is not Someone we can play with, or negotiate with. His greatness is not like the greatness of some mighty king whom we may defy in our minds and hearts, if not in our words and actions. On the contrary, God is so great that He knows all our thoughts. His greatness is infinitely beyond any earthly ruler we can imagine. He is an invisible and almighty Spirit whose presence should fill us with awe and fear, because 'our God is a consuming fire!' (Heb. 12:29). The Bible also calls Him 'the blessed and only Potentate, the King of kings and Lord of lords, who alone has immortality, dwelling in unapproachable light, whom no man has seen or can see, to whom be honour and everlasting power. Amen' (1 Tim. 6:15-16). Mortal, sinful men and women could get nearer to the heat and light of our fiery sun, than ever they could to the consuming fire and unapproachable light of God, the Holy One.

GOD IS ALSO UTTERLY SEPARATE FROM EVERYTHING IN HIS CHARACTER

God's holiness stems not only from the transcendent *greatness* of His being, but also from the moral *perfection* of His character. These two things set God apart from all other beings. The core concept of God's holiness, however, concerns His absolute purity which is absolutely intolerant of any form of sin, and therefore calls us as sinners to continual humility in His presence. Now the awe and fear of a supernatural being is common to all religions, but these other faiths do not have this moral or ethical dimension to their concept of deity. This is something quite distinctly biblical. The living and true God of the Bible cannot sin, hates sin and cannot tempt anyone to sin (Hab. 1:12-13; James 1:13; 1 John 1:5).

And once again the Israelites were taught this in two primary ways. In the first place, they were taught that the holiness that God requires of His people is *ethical* as well as ceremonial. To come before God in His temple was not simply a matter of wearing the right clothes and performing the right rituals and saying the right words. The God of the Bible demands that if people are going to have dealings with Him, they must be morally right before Him as well as ceremonially clean (Ps. 24:3-5). So right up front, as soon as the Jews came out of Egypt, God gave them the Ten Commandments (Exod. 20) with other moral rules amplifying the meaning of the Ten Commandments: rules governing their sexual conduct and bribes and witnessing against others, to specify just a few. Every area of life and behaviour had to be controlled by this code of holiness. In Leviticus 19:2 God says, 'You shall be holy [like this], for I the LORD your God am holy.' In other words, these are not just arbitrary rules that God has made up. They reflect the holiness of God's own moral character, and so He commands His people to reflect in some way that same moral trait of holiness.

The prophets majored on this theme. In Isaiah 33:14 we read, 'The sinners in Zion are afraid; fearfulness has seized the hypocrites: "Who among us shall dwell with the devouring fire? Who among us shall dwell with everlasting burnings?"' In verse 15 the answer given is, 'He who walks righteously and speaks uprightly, he who despises the gain of oppressions, who gestures with his hands, refusing bribes, who stops his ears from hearing of bloodshed, and shuts his eyes from seeing evil.' It is not merely the person who has offered the right sacrifices or performed the right rituals, but the person whose behaviour is morally right with God who 'shall dwell with the everlasting burnings'. However, it is impossible for sinners to live a life morally acceptable to God who is thrice holy, for we are born sinful (Ps. 51:5). And so the second way the moral dimension of God's holiness is highlighted in the Old Testament is its stress on the fact that men and women cannot come to God unless He atones for their sin. Thus when Isaiah has this tremendous experience of the holiness of God, his first reaction is one of utter dread. 'Woe is me', he says, 'for I am undone [literally, silenced as in death]! Because I am a man of unclean lips, and I dwell in the midst of a people of unclean lips; for my eyes have seen the King, the LORD of Hosts' (v. 5). His first response is to feel dirty, not for sins of deepest dye like murder, but for sinful speech (what we would reckon the least of sins).

And what is his salvation? How is he able to survive this encounter with God? He tells us that God sent a seraph (one of the angels) to purge away his sin with 'a live coal from the altar'. The altar in the forecourt of the temple in Jerusalem was the place where God commanded the blood of innocent animal victims to be shed in order to make atonement for the sins of the people. The seraph touched his mouth with a live coal from this altar and said, 'Behold, this has touched your lips; your iniquity is taken away, and your sin purged' (v. 7). That was the only way Isaiah, who knew he was morally unclean, could survive before an all-holy God. It was because God provided atonement for his sin. The Hebrew word translated 'purged' means 'to atone for'. The word literally means 'to cover' a debt or ransom price in order to secure a person's release. So then, God's holiness separates Himself from us, not because of His transcendent greatness alone, but also because of His moral perfection. These two things have to be kept together. We stand in awe and fear of God, not just because of the extraordinary majesty of His Person, but also because of His burning, all-consuming purity.

GOD'S HOLINESS BOTH REPELS AND DRAWS SINNERS

We have seen that this was the case for Isaiah. But is the thrice-holy God willing to receive all penitent sinners without distinction in the same way? Isaiah was at least trying to serve God as a prophet. Is there hope for people who sin persistently? This was a real problem in the Old Testament, because Israel was a nation of sinners whose sins only got worse and worse until in the end God sent them into captivity in Babylon, completely bereft of their temple and all their sacrifices. Could there be any hope for people under such divine judgment? The extraordinary thing is that the prophets God sent them said there was! Indeed, even more remarkable was the fact that these prophets said that there was hope for them because of the very holiness of God. The holiness of God which at first condemns sinners, then draws them to Himself in His mercy! Consider how this is expressed in Ezekiel 36 where God promises to redeem Israel from captivity:

Thus says the LORD God: 'I do not do this for your sake, O house of Israel, but for My holy name's sake, which you have profaned among the nations wherever you went ... and the nations shall know that I am the LORD ... when I am hallowed [seen to be holy] in you before their eyes. For I will take you from among the nations, gather you out of all countries, and bring you into your own land. Then I will sprinkle clean water on you, and you shall be clean; I will cleanse you from all your filthiness and from all your idols. I will give you a new heart and put a new spirit within you; I will take the heart of stone out of your flesh and give you a heart of flesh. I will put My Spirit within you and cause you to walk in My statutes, and you will keep My judgments and do them. Then you shall dwell in the land that I gave to your fathers; you shall be My people, and I will be your God. I will deliver you from all your uncleannesses' (vv. 22-29).

I wonder if we can understand how remarkable that is. God is going to make hopeless sinners holy, not for their sake primarily, but for His 'holy name's sake'. But how is He going to be able to do that without jeopardising His own holiness? If God is so morally perfect as we have seen, how can He gloss over such persistent sin? The Old Testament has no full answer to that. It just declares the certainty that sinners are going to be redeemed because God's holiness is not going to let sin have the last word. It is not until we get to the pages of the New Testament and the life and ministry of Jesus, the holy Lamb of God, that we can see how. Professor Mackintosh brings this out in an appealing way:

We can check our thought of the holiness of God by observing the holiness of Jesus. Here the same two-sided impression emerges. He was perfectly open-eyed about the evil in human life, and by being near Him men's eyes opened to its virulent presence in themselves. There is a dread, incidental severity in the two interjected words, 'if ye then, *being evil,* know how to give good gifts to your children' (Matt. vii. 11). His holiness burned with a scorching flame in which foul things were exposed and consumed. 'He told me all things that ever I did,' (John iv. 29) said one who had spent half an hour in His company. All this elicited in His associates the insight that they were unworthy to be in His presence. And yet that very holiness, by which they felt themselves judged, was seeking them from hour to hour. It was a condemning holiness; yes, but also it was a tender and merciful holiness, and it was essentially both. Precisely when men began to feel shame and to perceive the tragedy and hatefulness of their sin with sad-eyed clearness, just then it broke upon them, that Jesus was their friend. St. Peter sank down at His feet crying, 'Depart from me, for I am a sinful man'; but Jesus in response would not depart or withdraw His comradeship from the stricken man; instead He said, 'Fear not,' and kept Peter on beside Him (Luke v. 8-10). His attitude was at once so stern and so kind, so gentle and so unrelenting, that through Him the redemptive holiness of God touched and blessed their lives.[4]

The redemptive holiness of God, however, found its ultimate and supreme expression in the atoning death of our Lord Jesus Christ on the cross. There, as our sin-bearer, Jesus 'the Lamb of God who takes away the sin of the world' (John 1:29), bore the full penalty that God's law demanded and which the sins of His penitent, believing people deserve. No animal sacrifice could cover the debt of our sin (Heb. 10:4), only the blood of God (Acts 20:28). It is a great mystery we cannot fathom: how and why God in Christ was made

4. H.R. Macintosh, ibid, p. 171-172.

'sin for us, that we might become the righteousness of God in Him' (2 Cor. 5:19,21). It boggles our minds, but it is true! 'Salvation is of the LORD' (Jonah 2:9). Those who trust their soul to His mercy, will have the debt of their sin covered as Isaiah's was. Christ's death guarantees that. Nor will He let it rest there! He will put His Spirit within them and cause them to walk in His statutes for His holy name's sake (Ezek. 36:27).

> Not all the blood of beasts
> On Jewish altars slain,
> Could give the guilty conscience peace,
> Or wash away the stain:
>
> But Christ, the heav'nly Lamb,
> Takes all our sins away,
> A sacrifice of nobler name
> And richer blood than they.
>
> My faith would lay her hand
> On that dear head of Thine,
> While like a penitent I stand,
> And there confess my sin.
>
> My soul looks back to see
> The burdens Thou didst bear,
> When hanging on the cursed tree,
> And knows her guilt was there.
>
> Believing, we rejoice
> To see the curse remove;
> We bless the Lamb with cheerful voice,
> And sing His bleeding love.
>
> *(Isaac Watts, 1674-1748)*

10

THE LOVE OF GOD

The essence of love is the giving of self for the good of others. The truth that 'God is love' (1 John 4:8,16) means that it is His nature to eternally give of Himself in order to bestow blessing or good on others. Even before creation this attribute of God was active within the fellowship of the three persons of the Godhead. Thus in John 17:24 Jesus speaks to His Father of 'My glory which You have given Me, for You loved Me before the foundation of the world'. There was love and a giving of honour from the Father to the Son before time began. Moreover, the Son also loves the Father (John 14:31), and in the same manner we can assume that both the Father and the Son have an eternal love towards the Holy Spirit. The Father, the Son and the Holy Spirit always have enjoyed, and always will enjoy an endless life of mutual affection, honour and self-giving (Matt. 3:17; 17:5; John 3:35; 14:31; 16:13-15; 17:1-5,22-26).

The self-giving love of God within the Trinity is the same love that marks God's relationship to humankind despite our sinfulness, as the following Scriptures maintain:

For God so loved the world that He gave His only begotten Son, that whoever believes in Him should not perish but have everlasting life (John 3:16).

But God demonstrates His own love toward us, in that while we were still sinners, Christ died for us (Rom. 5:8).

... I live by faith in the Son of God, who loved me and gave Himself for me (Gal. 2:20).

In this the love of God was manifested toward us, that God has sent His only begotten Son into the world, that we might live through Him. In this is love, not that we loved God, but that He loved us and sent His Son *to* be the propitiation for our sins (1 John 4:9-10).

It should bring us to tears and godly repentance to know that it is the purpose of God the Father, Son and Holy Spirit to give themselves to the work of our redemption, in order to secure our eternal happiness; we who deserve nothing but eternal damnation for defying the Almighty.

Now there are some who deny that God is subject to emotional fluctuations like love or hate or joy or grief, because God is immutable: 'For I am the LORD, I do not change' (Mal. 3:6). It is true that the main Protestant Confessions or Articles of Faith assert that God is 'a most pure spirit, invisible, without body, parts or passions'. But in saying that God has no passions, they do not mean that God is unfeeling or impassive. Nor do they mean that there is nothing in Him that corresponds to the emotions and affections He put in us when He made us in His own image. For the Bible does speak of God's love for the world (John 3:16), and His grief because of human sinfulness (Gen. 6:5-6), and His joy over sinners who repent (Luke 15), and His pleasure when He saw what He had created (Gen. 1:31). It is an amazing truth in Scripture that God actually 'delights' in His people and 'rejoices over' them (Isa. 62:3-5; Zeph. 3:17-18).

What then did the framers of our Reformed Confessions mean when they said that God is 'without passions'? It is generally agreed by Reformed theologians that what they meant is that God's passions are not like our creaturely passions that are involuntary because they are aroused by circumstances that are not under our control, and because we are sinful they are also tainted by sin to some degree or another. So we speak of falling in love, or being provoked to anger, or being reduced to tears, or being surprised by joy, and so on. But that is not true of God. Emotions attributed to God in Scripture are the result of moral, wise, just and good choices on the part of God, and therefore voluntary and perfect attitudes to whatever He confronts and controls. Accordingly, to quote J.I. Packer, 'the love of the God who is spirit is no fitful, fluctuating thing, as the love of man is, nor is it a mere impotent longing for things that may never be; it is, rather, a spontaneous determination of God's whole being in an attitude of benevolence and benefaction, an attitude freely chosen and firmly fixed. There are no inconsistencies or vicissitudes in the love of the almighty God who is spirit. His love is "strong as death ... many waters cannot quench it" (Song, 8:6f.). Nothing can separate from it those whom it has once embraced (Rom. 8:35-39).'[1]

GOD'S LOVE IS A HOLY LOVE

The biblical revelation of God which distinguishes it from all other world religions is the staggering truth that 'God is love.' These three monosyllables occur twice in

1. J.I. Packer, *Knowing God*, p. 110.

the First Epistle of John (1 John 4:8,16). Although God's love is referred to many times throughout Scripture, it is only here that the statement 'God is love' is made so baldly. In doing so the apostle is not simply saying that God is a God who loves, but that He is love itself. Whatever God does in creation is motivated and directed by His self-giving for the blessing of others. It is the divine motive behind creation and redemption. Of course, we must be careful not to misinterpret this tremendous and vital truth. John is not saying that God is only love, or that God has nothing but love in His character. Unfortunately, this is how many people have misunderstood these great words. They believe that the only thing anyone can say about God is that He is love. But we only have to look around at all the misery and pain that is in the world to know that love is not the only side to God's character. Indeed, this has caused many people to question whether God is love, and they would be quite right if these words of John meant that God is all love. How could a God who is all love allow death and disease and wars and crime and natural calamities to bring such suffering on people all over the world? Either he is not almighty and unable to do anything to rid the world of these miseries; or He is not all love, and so many people want nothing to do with the Bible and the God it proclaims.

The problem, however, is not with who God is, but with the false ideas that men and women have of Him. For God is not all love. There is another side to God's character that John has already highlighted in chapter 1 when he says, 'God is light' (1 John 1:5). 'Light' in the Bible is a symbol of holiness and 'darkness' is a symbol of evil. Thus John adds the explanatory statement: 'and in Him is no darkness at all' (see also John 3:19-21; 8:12; Eph. 5:8,11). By the phrase, 'God is light', John is saying that God is holy and just as well as love. Indeed, God is *holy love,* and He will not allow sin or evil to go unpunished. The God who is love created Adam and Eve, gave them the loveliest garden the world has ever seen, and came at the end of each day to enjoy fellowship with them. But when they sinned, He put them out of the garden, took away their access to 'the tree of life', and pronounced upon them the curse of sin, which is death (Gen. 2:8-10,16-17; 3:22-24).

Sixteen hundred years later, the same God who is love destroyed the whole human race by means of a flood, because their wickedness was so great. He spared only Noah and his family. The apostle John himself witnessed God's righteous judgment upon his own nation when Jerusalem and its temple were destroyed by the Romans, twenty years before he wrote his First Epistle (Matt. 24:1-2). One day, it could be in our generation, God (who is holy love) is going to come in the Person of His Son, Jesus Christ, to judge the world in righteousness (Matt. 24:3-31; 2 Thess. 1:6-10). So while it is not true to say that God is all love, at the same time it needs to be said that God is love in a far more fundamental sense than He is wrathful.

In fact, one can hardly imagine the Bible saying: 'God is wrath' in quite the same sense it says, 'God is love.' Indeed, Scripture itself describes God's wrath and destruction of His enemies as 'His strange work ... His strange act' (Isa. 28:21, KJV; NKJV has 'His unusual act'; margin reads, 'literally *foreign')*. In other words, wrath or anger do not reside in God's heart as an eternally active emotion. God's wrath is unusual, because it can only be aroused by sin and appeased or propitiated when that sin is punished and His justice satisfied. God's anger, therefore, is a temporary emotion, whereas His love is a permanent emotion.

There never was a time when God was not love, but there was a time when He was not angry. Before sin entered the world anger was not active in the heart of God, because there was no sin to be angry about. Throughout that endless past eternity, perfect love was freely and fully expressed between the Father and the Son and the Holy Spirit in the Godhead. And so while it is not true to say that God is all love, it is certainly true to say that perfect love is an eternal, primary, active attribute of His glorious character. That ought to greatly quicken our anticipation of heaven, where the redeemed will share forever in the joyful give-and-take of the divine love relationship Christ has won for us, and where there will be no sin and no divine wrath ever again forever (Rev. 21,22). 'Perfect love casts out fear' (1 John 4:18).

GOD HAS A GENERAL LOVE
FOR EVERYBODY

The term theologians have given to this truth is 'common grace'. God is good to everybody, irrespective of their spiritual condition. His universal kindness is attested to in many Scriptures. In Psalm 145 David says, 'The LORD is gracious and compassionate, slow to anger and rich in love. The LORD is good to all; He has compassion on all He has made … The eyes of all look to You, and You give them their food at the proper time. You open Your hand and satisfy the desires of every living thing' (vv. 8-9,15-16, NIV). Our Lord Jesus makes a similar point when He says that God 'is kind to the unthankful and evil. Therefore be merciful, just as Your Father also is merciful' (Luke 6:35-36); and again in Matthew 5:45, 'Your Father in heaven … makes His sun to rise on the evil and on the good, and sends rain on the just and on the unjust.' Without sunshine and rain there could be no harvest anywhere. But when God sends rain it falls on the whole community. It does not just water the Christian's garden, leaving the unbeliever's ground parched like a desert. And when the sun shines, it beams its life-giving rays on the crops of saints and sinners alike. God is good to all! Not only in money and material possessions, but in many other gracious gifts that gladden our daily lives, like family life. 'He who finds a wife finds a good thing, and obtains favour from the LORD,' says Proverbs 18:22. 'Children are a heritage of the LORD, and the fruit of the womb is His reward,' says Psalm 127:3. These joys are not confined to Christians. Marriage is a gift of creation and children a gift of providence. They are comforts given to all humankind, including unbelievers. Mental and artistic abilities are also gifts of common grace. They do not depend upon our moral and spiritual condition.

These, plus countless other good gifts, are expressions of God's general love for everybody. And it is because God loves everybody like that, that He expects Christians to do the same. He says, 'Love your enemies, bless those who curse you, do good to those who hate you, and pray for those who spitefully use you and persecute you, that you may be sons of your Father in heaven; for He makes His sun rise on the evil and on the good, and sends rain on the just and on the unjust' (Matt. 5:44-45). God has a general love for all men and women.

GOD HAS A SPECIAL LOVE FOR HIS CHOSEN PEOPLE

In Ephesians 1 Paul says, 'Blessed be the God and Father of our Lord Jesus Christ, who ... chose us in Him before the foundation of the world, that we should be holy and blameless before Him. In love He predestined us for adoption as sons through Jesus Christ, according to the purpose of His will' (vv. 3-5, ESV). Many find fault with this and say it smacks of favouritism. But our objection to God's sovereign right to adopt into His family those whom He chooses is sheer arrogance. How dare we think that we can tell God how many children He should adopt, when we jealously reserve that very right for ourselves? It is incredible that God should want any of us to live forever with Him in heaven. The Bible says we are 'haters of God, violent, proud, boasters, inventors of evil things, disobedient to parents, undiscerning, untrustworthy, unloving, unforgiving, unmerciful; who, knowing the righteous judgment of God, that those who practise such things are deserving of death, not only do the same but also approve of those who practise them' (Rom. 1:30-32). There is nothing whatever in any of us as sinners to call forth God's love; nothing to attract Him to us. We are vile and full of sin.

Yet in the matchless greatness of His love, God has freely, spontaneously and without cause, chosen to redeem a people for Himself whom no man can number (Gen. 22:15-18; Rom. 9:6-8; Gal. 3:7-9; Rev. 7:9-10). The only reason God chose to love any sinner at all, Scripture says, is because it was His sovereign good pleasure to do so (Eph. 1:4-5). This is true both in terms of His natural and spiritual blessings to us. Why are we living in peace and prosperity in the Western World, when millions are dying of war and starvation and political oppression? It is only the result of God's good will. The average Westerner does not find fault with God for that! Nor with the fact that we have enjoyed the light of the gospel for many hundreds of years, whereas other countries have not heard it at all. How do we account for that? It is not because we have deserved such an outpouring of God's special love, because we have not. All countries and all nations alike deserve only God's wrath, because all human beings are sinners (enemies) who feel no gratitude for all His mercies (Rom. 1:20-21; 3:23). There is no explanation, except that God is free to bestow His special love on whom He chooses.

God's dealings with Pharaoh when he would not let Israel leave Egypt is a classic example, one which the apostle Paul uses in Romans 9:14-18, 'What shall we say then? Is there unrighteousness with God? Certainly not! For He says to Moses, "I will have mercy on whomever I will have mercy, and I will have compassion on whomever I will have compassion." So then it is not of him who wills, nor of him who runs, but of God who shows mercy. For the Scripture says to the Pharaoh, "For this very purpose I have raised you up, that I may show My power in you, and that My name may be declared in all the earth." Therefore He has mercy on whom He wills, and whom He wills He hardens.'

Is God unjust to choose some for salvation (the Israelites) and abandon others (the Egyptians)? That is the question Paul is addressing in Romans 9:14-18, and this is how John Stott sums up the apostle's answer:

> So God is not unjust. The fact is, as Paul demonstrated in the early chapters of his letter, that all human beings are sinful and guilty in God's sight (3:9,19), so that nobody deserves to be saved. If therefore God hardens some, he is not being unjust, for that is what their sin deserves. If, on the other hand, he has compassion on some, he is not being unjust, for he is dealing with them in mercy. The wonder is not that some are saved and others not, but that anybody is saved at all. For we deserve nothing at God's hand but judgment. If we receive what we deserve (which is judgment), or if we

receive what we do not deserve (which is mercy), in neither case is God unjust. If therefore anybody is lost, the blame is theirs, but if anybody is saved, the credit is God's. This antinomy contains a mystery which our present knowledge cannot solve; but it is consistent with Scripture, history and experience.[2]

The whole Bible teaches this. In Deuteronomy 10:15 Moses makes much of the free, special love that God showed to His chosen people in the Old Testament. He says, 'Yet the LORD set His heart in love on your fathers and chose their offspring after them, you above all peoples, as you are this day' (ESV). The same assurance is given to the Christian church who are God's chosen people in the New Testament. In Acts 20 it is called 'the church of God which He purchased with His own blood' (v. 28). In 1 John 4:9-10 the apostle says, 'In this the love of God was manifested toward us, that God has sent His only begotten Son into the world, that we might live through Him. In this is love, not that we loved God, but that He loved us and sent His Son to be the propitiation for our sins.' In verse 19 he writes, 'We love Him because He first loved us.'

The Bible never gives a human reason why God has chosen believing Jews and Gentiles throughout history to be a people for Himself, because 'all have sinned and fall short of the glory of God' (Rom. 3:23). There is no merit or virtue in any human being that could deserve or earn the favour of God. Without Christ we all stand 'condemned' by the holy law of God, and all 'boasting' is 'excluded' (John 3:18-19; Rom. 3:27). Thus God said to Israel through Moses: 'For you are a holy people to the LORD your God; the LORD your God has chosen you to be a people for Himself, a special treasure above all the peoples on the face of the earth. The LORD did

---

2. John Stott, *Romans* (Inter-Varsity Press, 1994), pp. 269-270.

not set His love on you nor choose you because you were more in number than any other people, for you were the least of all peoples; but because the LORD loves you, and because He would keep the oath which He swore to your fathers, the LORD has brought you out with a mighty hand, and redeemed you from the house of bondage, from the hand of Pharaoh king of Egypt' (Deut. 7:6-8).

For New Testament believers, Paul has this sobering reminder: 'For you see your calling, brethren, that not many wise according to the flesh, not many mighty, not many noble, are called. But God has chosen the foolish things of the world to put to shame the wise, and God has chosen the weak things of the world to put to shame the things which are mighty; and the base things of the world and the things which are despised God has chosen, and the things which are not, to bring to nothing the things that are, that no flesh should glory in His presence' (1 Cor. 1:26-29). There was absolutely nothing in us to attract the heart of God. His love for unlovable wretches like us was free, spontaneous and unevoked. Blessed be His name!

GOD'S LOVE FOR HIS OWN IS ETERNAL

Because God is eternal, His love for those whom He has chosen began in eternity past. In Jeremiah 31:3 God says to all His believing people, 'I have loved you with an everlasting love; therefore with lovingkindness I have drawn you.' The same thing is said of Jesus and His followers: 'When Jesus knew that His hour had come that He should depart from this world to the Father, having loved His own who were in the world, He loved them to the end' (John 13:1). Paul in Romans 8:38-39 also assures us of the irrevocable love of God: 'For I am persuaded that neither death nor life, nor angels nor principalities nor powers, nor things present nor things to come, nor height nor depth, nor any other created thing, shall be able to separate us from the love of God which is in Christ Jesus our Lord.' Having chosen us from 'before the foundation of the world' (Eph. 1:4), God's love is fixed upon us. It is immutable because God is immutable. Thus Paul can say, 'But we are bound to give thanks to God always for you, brethren beloved by the Lord, because God from the beginning chose you for salvation through sanctification by the Spirit and belief in the truth' (2 Thess. 2:13).

C.H. Spurgeon, with his usual flourish, comments:

In the very beginning, when this great universe lay in the mind of God, like unborn forests in the acorn cup; long ere the echoes awoke the solitudes; before the mountains were brought forth; and long ere the light flashed through the sky, God loved His chosen creatures. Before there was any created being – when the ether was not fanned by an angel's wing, when space itself had not an existence, where there was nothing save God alone – even then, in that loneliness of Deity, and in that deep quiet and profundity, His bowels moved with love for His chosen. Their names were written on His heart, and then were they dear to His soul. Jesus loved His people before the foundation of the world – even from eternity! and when He called me by His grace, He said to me, 'I have loved *thee* with an everlasting love: therefore with lovingkindness have I drawn thee.[3]

The book of Hosea brings out God's endless love for His people in a very poignant way. Having been previously separated, the prophet Hosea was commanded by God to pursue his estranged wife Gomer whom he bought back from a slave auction (Hosea 3:1-2). In the early

---

3. C.H. Spurgeon, *Autobiography* (Banner of Truth, 1973), vol. 1, p. 167.

days of their marriage she bore him a son, but the next two children were fathered by adulterous affairs (1:3,6,8). Hosea's marriage was to mirror the spiritual infidelity of God's people Israel, and how God would continue to love them 'for better, for worse'. The story reaches its climax in chapter 11. Here God's love, typified by Hosea taking Gomer back, extends even to the rebellious illegitimate children of the marriage, something almost unthinkable in any marriage. But such was God's loyal love for His covenant people, in spite of their idolatry. Thus He says, 'When Israel was a child, I loved him, and out of Egypt I called My son. But the more I called Israel, the further they went from Me. They sacrificed to the Baals and they burned incense to images. It was I who taught Ephraim to walk, taking them by the arms; but they did not realize it was I who healed them. I led them with cords of human kindness, with ties of love. I lifted the yoke from their neck, and bent down to feed them' (Hosea 11:1-4, NIV).

There is immense feeling in these verses; a sense of injury and disappointment. The God who truly loves His own is not unfeeling or impassive. And here in Hosea 11 He is portrayed as a Father who remembers with tenderness and joy how He taught His child to 'walk'. How He 'healed' their scratches, and drew them 'with ties of love', and relieved them of burdens that were too heavy to bear, and how He 'bent down to feed them'. And yet, says God, 'the more I called Israel, the further they went from Me.' But divine love never gives up. God is committed to win them back by loving chastisement. Gomer, too, was disciplined; she was denied conjugal rights for 'many days' (3:3). True love is tough love (Prov. 3:11-12; Heb. 12:5-6). So God says in Hosea 11:5, 'He [Israel] shall not return to the land of Egypt; but the Assyrian shall be his king, because they refused to repent.' God is not giving up on them. He cannot, because He is God and His love for His own is eternal: 'How can I give you up, Ephraim? How can I hand you over, Israel? How can I make you like Admah? How can I set you like Zeboiim? My heart churns within Me; My sympathy is stirred. I will not execute the fierceness of My anger; I will not again destroy Ephraim. For I am God, and not man, the Holy One in your midst; and I will not come with terror' (vv. 8-9). What a wonderful picture of God's unfailing love for His people. As Paul puts it: 'If we are faithless, He remains faithful; He cannot deny Himself' (2 Tim. 2:13).

Nowhere, however, is God's love more fully portrayed than on the cross of Calvary where Jesus Christ bore the guilt and punishment of the sins of those who trust Him for salvation (Matt. 26:28; John 1:29; Gal. 3:13; 1 Pet. 2:24; 3:18). 'In this is love,' says John, 'not that we loved God, but that He loved us and sent His Son to be the propitiation for our sins' (1 John 4:10). And Paul says, 'God demonstrates His own love toward us, in that while we were still sinners, Christ died for us' (Rom. 5:8). How humble and grateful we should be that we have a God of love like that!

If we are strangers to that love, let us know that to turn our backs persistently upon God's love is the greatest sin of all. It is the unpardonable sin, because it resists the Holy Spirit's work of bringing sinners to Christ (Matt. 12:31-32). We may think at the moment that the devil has more to offer, but he has not. All that we may prize above God now is only temporal. It will turn to ashes in the end (2 Pet. 3:10). We need to come to Christ in repentance and faith while we can, for it is only through Christ that we can be reconciled to God and become one of His adopted children (2 Cor. 5:18-21).

If we are Christians, let us take heart from the fact that 'God is love.' For as A.W. Pink wisely reminds us:

> Here then is abundant cause for trust and patience under Divine affliction. Christ was beloved of the Father, yet *He* was not exempted from poverty, disgrace, and persecution. *He* hungered and thirsted. Thus, it was *not* incompatible with God's *love* for Christ when He permitted men to spit upon and smite Him. Then let no Christian call into question God's love when he is brought under painful afflictions and trials. God did not enrich Christ on earth with temporal prosperity, for 'He had not where to lay His head.' But He *did* give Him the Spirit "without measure" (John 3:34). Learn then that *spiritual* blessings are the principal gifts of Divine love. How blessed to know that when the world hates us, God loves us![4]

The love of God is greater far
Than tongue or pen can ever tell;
It goes beyond the highest star,
And reaches to the lowest hell,
The guilty pair, bowed down with care,
God gave His Son to win;
His erring child He reconciled,
And pardoned from his sin.

O love of God, how rich and pure!
How measureless and strong!
It shall for evermore endure –
The saints' and angels' song.

Could we with ink the ocean fill,
And were the skies of parchment made,
Were every stalk on earth a quill,

---

4. A.W. Pink, *The Attributes of God*, p. 81

And every man a scribe by trade;
To write the love of God above
Would drain the ocean dry;
Nor could the scroll contain the whole.
Tho' stretched from sky to sky.

(Frederick M. Lehman, 1868-1953)

11

THE GRACE AND MERCY OF GOD

The living and true God of the Bible is both infinitely holy and good. In the words of the apostle John, 'God is light' (1 John 1:5) and 'God is love' (1 John 4:8,16). God's holiness is so majestic that He is described as 'dwelling in unapproachable light, whom no man has seen or can see' (1 Tim. 6:16). God's love in giving Christ for us is called an 'indescribable gift' (2 Cor. 9:15), because 'God so loved the world [the ungodly] that He gave His only begotten Son [as an atoning sacrifice], that whoever believes in Him should not perish but have everlasting life' (John 3:16; cf. Rom. 5:6,8; 1 John 4:8-10). Thus it is right to say that the holiness of God awes us, but the love of God draws us. This is particularly true when God's love for a world of sinners is further broken down in Scripture into two other attributes that are closely related: namely, God's grace and His mercy.

THE NATURE OF GOD'S GRACE
AND MERCY

Grace and mercy are used almost interchangeably in the Bible, but there is a difference that is helpful to note as far as our understanding is concerned. Grace is one of the most important words in the New Testament. We cannot understand the Christian Faith without knowing the meaning of 'grace', for the God of Christianity is 'the God of all grace' (1 Pet. 5:10); the Holy Spirit is 'the Spirit of grace' (Heb. 10:29); and 'grace and truth came through Jesus Christ' (John 1:17). Little wonder that the word 'grace' occurs more than one hundred and fifty times, and more than one hundred and thirty of them come from the pen of the apostle Paul. He was the great herald of grace who could say: 'Chains and tribulations await me. But none of these things move me; nor do I count my life dear to myself, so that I may finish my race with joy, and the ministry which I received from the Lord Jesus, to testify to the gospel of the grace of God' (Acts 20:23-24).

Now the Greek word in the New Testament for 'grace' is *charis* and it means a 'gift' or 'favour' bestowed by a superior upon someone who is undeserving. In Luke 1:28 the angel Gabriel addresses the virgin Mary as 'highly favoured' because, although she was a sinner like everyone else, God had chosen her to be the mother of the Saviour of the world (vv. 31-33). That is the picture. Grace is the unsought, unearned and unmerited favour of God bestowed on sinful men and women who, but for His spontaneous, self-determined love, deserve only punishment. The mercy of God, on the other hand, is the effect of God's goodness helping the helpless in their misery and distress. Grace is the heart of God prompted to bestow blessing on the guilty, mercy is the hand of God that proffers the blessing on them in their helplessness (Ps. 103:8,11; Micah 7:18-20; 2 Cor. 1:3; James 2:13). To take the distinction a bit further: it is because God is, in the words of Scripture, 'the God of all grace', that sinners can appeal to Him to have mercy upon them and save them. Only a gracious God can be a merciful God. Grace is inward, issuing in a favourable disposition to hell-deserving sinners; mercy is outward, issuing in God's salvation of helpless sinners (Rom. 5:6-8).

The two terms carry the combined meaning of bestowing favour and blessing on sinners who deserve only judgment and divine wrath. A good example is Exodus 33:19 where God says, 'I will be gracious to whom I will be gracious, and I will show mercy on whom I will show mercy' (ESV). They are parallel statements. Ephesians 2:4-5 is another example. Paul says, 'But God who is rich in mercy because of His great love with which He loved us, even when we were dead in trespasses, made us alive together with Christ (by grace you have been saved).' Regeneration is attributed to both. Again, Titus 2:11 says, 'the grace of God brings salvation,' whereas Titus 3:4-5 says, 'When the kindness and the love of God our Saviour toward man appeared ... according to His mercy He saved us.' To sum up the distinction once more, God's grace is the source of His mercy, and God's mercy is the response of His grace. God's grace is always the fountain of His mercy.

OUR NEED OF GOD'S GRACE
AND MERCY

Human depravity
The New Testament doctrine of grace presupposes universal human sin and guilt. Throughout Scripture sin is a moral corruption found at every point in every man and woman, and variously described as transgressing God's law, missing the mark of ethical perfection God has set for us, and thereby incurring guilt before our divine Judge (Gen. 6:5; Ps. 51:5;

1 Kings 8:46; Rom. 3:9-23; 7:18; 1 John 1:8-10). This God-defying, self-serving character trait affects our thoughts and desires, and at root is a spirit of pride and rebellion against God. It is the same spirit that is seen in Adam and Eve's disobedience in the Garden of Eden. The fact that there is no part of our being unaffected by sin means that there is nothing in us or our actions that can earn or merit God's favour. Unless we are saved by grace, we have no hope of heaven when we die (John 3:15-19; Titus 2:11-14; 3:4-7).

The average person in the street will not accept the biblical view of the moral and spiritual state of human nature. It is too humbling and unpalatable. For as J.I. Packer explains:

> Modern man, conscious of his tremendous scientific achievements in recent years, naturally inclines to a high opinion of himself. He views material wealth as in any case more important than moral character, and in the moral realm he is resolutely kind to himself, treating small virtues as compensating for great vices and refusing to take seriously the idea that, morally speaking, there is anything much wrong with him. He tends to dismiss a bad conscience, in himself as in others, as an unhealthy psychological freak, a sign of disease and mental aberration rather than an index of moral reality. For modern man is convinced that, despite all his little peccadilloes – drinking, gambling, reckless driving, 'fiddling', black and white lies, sharp practice in trading, dirty reading, and what have you – he is at heart a thoroughly good fellow. Then, as pagans do (and modern man's heart is pagan – make no mistake about that), he imagines God as a magnified image of himself, and assumes that God shares his own complacency about himself. The thought of himself as a creature fallen from God's image, a rebel against God's rule, guilty and unclean

in God's sight, fit only for God's condemnation, never enters his head.[1]

Human depravity, however, is not something we can turn a blind eye to. We are not sinners because we sin, but rather we sin because we are sinners, born with a sinful nature (Job 14:4; Ps. 51:5; 58:3; John 3:6; Rom. 5:12). Thus God requires perfection. One sin throughout our whole life is one too many. It is enough to keep us out of heaven, because it is proof that our heart is evil. Given time and the right circumstances all of us will only become more sinful, just as an apple with only one worm in it will eventually become altogether rotten. In Romans 3 Paul quotes from various Old Testament scriptures to show that in God's eyes humankind is universally evil: 'There is none righteous; no, not one ... there is none who seeks after God. They have all turned aside ... there is none who does good, no, not one ... with their tongues they have practised deceit ... their feet are swift to shed blood ... there is no fear of God before their eyes' (vv. 10-18). The last book of the Bible says, 'There shall by no means enter it [heaven] anything that defiles, or causes an abomination or a lie, but only those who are written in the Lamb's Book of Life' (Rev. 21:27). That means that every last one of us is not only undeserving of heaven, but thoroughly and justly deserving of everlasting hell. God cannot be true to Himself unless He punishes sin in the way it deserves. And until we know and feel the truth of this fact, we will never desire or appreciate God's grace and mercy.

Human inability

Total depravity, however, is not the only moral factor hindering men and women from seeing their need of

---

1. J.I. Packer, *Knowing God*, pp. 117-118.

God's grace and mercy. Connected to human depravity is human inability or unwillingness to turn to the living and true God in repentance and faith. Man is a free agent who can choose whatever he likes. What he likes, however, does not include the God of the Bible. He has an inherent aversion towards God. Although he was created to worship God, man in his spiritual rebellion worships only the gods of his choosing, however irrational. All the false religions are man-made and built on the belief that man can appease his gods and win their favour with suitable sacrifices of his own choosing and making. Even some church people believe that simply going to church and trying to live a respectable life will ensure a place for them in heaven. But a humanly respectable life is not perfection. It will not pass divine inspection: 'Can the Ethiopian change his skin or the leopard its spots? Then you may also do good, who are accustomed to do evil' (Jer. 13:23). Isaiah 64:5-6 says, 'You are indeed angry, for we have sinned – in these ways we continue; and we need to be saved. But we are all like an unclean thing, and all our righteousnesses are like filthy rags.'

'Therefore', says Paul, 'by the deeds of the law no flesh will be justified in His sight' (Rom. 3:20). In its spiritual helplessness, the human race was utterly dependent upon God's grace and mercy to redeem them. And this He did, despite our demerit: 'For when we were still without strength, in due time Christ died for the ungodly. For scarcely for a righteous man will one die; yet perhaps for a good man someone would even dare to die. But God demonstrates His own love toward us, in that while we were still sinners, Christ died for us' (Rom. 5:6-8). There was no sacrifice man could offer to atone for his sin and satisfy God's justice. It had to be a sacrifice of infinite worth to cover humanity's offences against an infinitely holy God. But God, being the merciful God that He is, took the initiative and offered Himself, in the person of His Son, to be that sacrifice for our sin. On the cross of Calvary it was God in Christ reconciling the world to Himself (2 Cor. 5:18-21; see also Gal. 3:13; 1 Pet. 3:18). Total depravity entails total inability. We cannot earn God's favour, no matter what we do. Nothing but free, sovereign divine grace and mercy can save us from eternal punishment (Matt. 25:46).

> Not the labours of my hands
> Can fulfil Thy law's demands:
> Could my zeal no respite know,
> Could my tears for ever flow,
> All for sin could not atone;
> Thou must save, and Thou alone.
>
> *(A.M. Toplady, 1740-1778)*

THE BLESSINGS OF GOD'S GRACE
AND MERCY

As finite creatures we often find ourselves in the position where we sincerely and desperately want to help others but cannot for lack of resources or opportunity or authority. That, however, never applies to God who is almighty and has infinite resources. Scripture therefore speaks of 'God who is rich in mercy' (Eph. 2:4) and having 'abundant mercy' (Ps. 86:5; 1 Pet. 1:3), and of 'the riches of His grace' (Eph. 1:7), indeed of 'the exceeding riches of His grace' (Eph. 2:7). But what are the 'riches' that God in His grace and mercy through Christ is willing to lavish on unlovely, ill-deserving perishing sinners? Primarily they are not material and temporal, but spiritual and eternal. They are the blessings of salvation, and that is why the gospel (which means good news) is called both 'the gospel of salvation' and 'the gospel of the grace of God' (Eph. 1:13; Acts 20:24). It is also called 'the glorious gospel of the blessed God … [which] is worthy of all acceptance, that Christ Jesus came into the world to save sinners' (1 Tim. 1:11,15). What are the blessings of salvation?

The forgiveness of sins

The gospel is the good news that God our Judge has become our Saviour. But to do so, He had to become one of us. He took our flesh when He was miraculously conceived by the Holy Spirit in the womb of the virgin Mary (Matt. 1:20-23; Luke 1:26-35). He identified Himself with us in every respect except our fallen and sinful human nature, so that He could be an acceptable 'mediator between God and men' (1 Tim. 2:5). Sin has estranged humankind from God and Jesus Christ had to be truly both human and divine in order to identify with and maintain the interests of each party as a go-between. After a sinless life of 30 years or more, Jesus went to the cross of Calvary to 'make His soul an offering for sin' (Isa. 53:10; Phil. 2:5-8). By His penal substitutionary death 'He [God] made Him who knew no sin to be sin for us, that we might become the righteousness of God in Him' (2 Cor. 5:21). That is the first blessing of God's gracious salvation. 'In Him', says Paul, 'we have redemption through His blood, the forgiveness of our sins, according to the riches of His grace.' What an enormous blessing it is to have all our sins (past, present and future) washed away by the blood of the 'Lamb of God who takes away the sin of the world' (John 1:29; 1 John 1:7-9), and to have peace with God! 'God was in Christ, reconciling the world to Himself, not imputing their trespasses to them,' but imputing them to Christ in our stead (2 Cor. 5:19-21). And now we can sing,

Before the throne of God above
I have a strong and perfect plea.
A great high Priest whose Name is Love
Who ever lives and pleads for me.
My name is graven on His hands,
My name is written on His heart.
I know that while in Heaven He stands
No tongue can bid me thence depart.

When Satan tempts me to despair
And tells me of the guilt within,
Upward I look and see Him there
Who made an end of all my sin.
Because the sinless Saviour died
My sinful soul is counted free.
For God the just is satisfied
To look on Him and pardon me.

Behold Him there the risen Lamb,
My perfect spotless righteousness,
The great unchangeable I AM,
The King of glory and of grace,
One with Himself I cannot die.
My soul is purchased by His blood,
My life is hid with Christ on high,
With Christ my Saviour and my God!

(Charitie L. Bancroft, 1841-1923)

The gift of the Holy Spirit

In his sermon on the Day of Pentecost, Peter said to the crowd in Jerusalem, 'Repent, and let every one of you be baptised in the name of Jesus Christ for the remission of sins; and you shall receive the gift of the Holy Spirit' (Acts 2:38). The blessings of salvation do not stop with the forgiveness of our sins and reconciliation with God. Something has to be done to free us from sin; to deliver us from its power and eventually from its very presence. God needs to change our sinful nature and give us a passion for 'holiness without which no man shall see the Lord' (Heb. 12:14). This blessing is called the 'baptism' or 'gift' of the Holy Spirit (Acts 1:5; 2:38). In the same moment that God forgives our sin, He baptises us with the Spirit, and water baptism is the sacred sign of the miraculous change that takes place in us by the power of the Holy Spirit. Salvation is not parcelled out bit by bit. Pardon, reconciliation and regeneration all occur instantaneously. So to receive the Holy Spirit is to receive 'power from on high' (Luke 24:49); to 'be born again'; to become 'a new creature in Christ Jesus'; and to be His 'witnesses' (John 3:3-7; 2 Cor. 5:17; Acts 1:8).

In addition, by the miraculous event of regeneration, believers are given the power of sanctification. That is to say, the power to hate sin and resist it. To quote Paul again, 'The law of the Spirit of life in Christ Jesus has made me free from the law of sin and death' (Rom. 8:1-2). And again, 'Walk in the Spirit, and you shall not fulfil the lust of the flesh' (Gal. 5:16-17). To help us in our walk with God, we also receive the grace of illumination. Before coming to Christ, we walked in spiritual darkness (Eph. 5:8; 1 Cor. 2:14). The Bible was a closed book and God's will was unknown to us. But when we became Christians we 'received, not the spirit of the world, but the Spirit who is from God, that we might know the things that have been freely given to us by God' (1 Cor. 2:12). What a wonderful blessing to have 'the Spirit of grace' (Heb. 10:29) Himself dwelling in us as the Spirit of illumination who helps us 'grow in the grace and knowledge of our Lord and Saviour, Jesus Christ' (2 Pet. 3:18). The blessings of God's grace just go on and on. In Ephesians 1:3 Paul bursts into praise for them, saying, 'Blessed be the God and Father of our Lord Jesus Christ, who has blessed us with every spiritual blessing [or every blessing of the Spirit] in the heavenly places [or realm of spiritual reality] in Christ.' There is not one blessing that we need to live a God-honouring, Christ-exalting life, that is not ours to enjoy and benefit from in the gift of the Holy Spirit, who is also called 'the Spirit of Christ' (Rom. 8:9).

Let me, however, highlight just one more of these blessings, and that is the Holy Spirit's ministry of sealing God's purchase of our lives and thereby guaranteeing our final redemption. For in Ephesians 1:13-14 Paul says, 'In Him you also trusted, after you heard the word of truth, the gospel of your salvation; in whom also, having believed, you were sealed with the Holy Spirit of promise, who is the guarantee of our inheritance until the redemption of the purchased possession, to the praise of His glory.' When we put our trust in Christ for salvation, God seals us with the gift of the Holy Spirit. Now, a seal is a mark of ownership. In New Testament days slaves were branded with a seal to mark whom they belonged to. Likewise, the mark of a Christian that brands him or her as belonging to God, is the gift of the Holy Spirit who indwells them. This sealing is not something the Holy Spirit does. The seal is the Holy Spirit Himself. So if someone does not have the Holy Spirit dwelling in them, they do not belong to God (Rom. 8:9). The apostle then elaborates on this by saying that the Holy Spirit is thereby 'the guarantee' of our inheritance (v. 14).

In other words, He is God's pledge to bring us safe at last to glory. The Greek word translated 'guarantee' literally means an 'earnest' (KJV) or down-payment given as proof of our commitment to purchase something. The guarantee is not something different from what is guaranteed. It is itself a part of the payment, and it is called the 'earnest-money'. In the same way, God gives us the Holy Spirit as the first instalment of our salvation. For to have the fellowship of the Holy Spirit during our short life on earth is a wonderful foretaste of the full communion we will have with the Triune God in heaven forever. When we believe in Christ, we become God's purchased possession. He is not going to give up on the transaction He has begun by giving us the Holy Spirit (1 Cor. 6:19-20). His grace will see the transaction through to the end (our glorification).

How does this precious truth affect us if we have not yet come to Christ in repentance and faith? It should be a warning not to presume on the goodness of a God who is merciful, gracious and longsuffering. The only attribute of God that is not infinite is His patience. Patience can only be a virtue if it is exhaustible. It is a good thing to be slow to anger, but it is not a good thing to be incapable of anger altogether. If God were to go on tolerating our rebellion and impenitence forever, He would have no moral character at all. Indeed, His forbearance would be a sign of moral indifference. 'I do not frustrate the grace of God ...', says Paul (Gal. 2:21, KJV). We must not think that God is too merciful to send anyone to hell. If that were true, hell would be empty, which it is not. On the contrary, God is a God of justice as well as mercy, who by His own mouth says He will 'by no means clear the guilty' (Exod. 34:7; Num. 14:18). Thus Paul solemnly warns us: 'Do you think ... that you will escape the judgment of God? Or do you despise the riches of His goodness, forbearance and longsuffering, not knowing that the goodness of God leads you to repentance?' (Rom. 2:3-4). At least that is its purpose. By continuing to resist God's grace and forbearance, we are only multiplying sin upon sin, and heaping up God's wrath against ourselves. Let us beware of the fury of a patient God and respond positively to His grace and mercy in Christ. Let us come to Jesus now in repentance and faith, and cast ourselves upon His grace and mercy to forgive all our sins and fill our life with His Holy Spirit.

If we are Christians, let us so live that, like Paul, we can say: 'By the grace of God I am what I am, and His grace toward me was not in vain; but I laboured more abundantly than they all, yet not I, but the grace of God which was with me' (1 Cor. 15:10).

When Dr. William Carey was suffering from a dangerous illness, he was asked, 'If this sickness proves fatal, what passage would you select as the text for your funeral sermon?' He replied, 'Oh, I feel that such a poor, sinful creature is unworthy to have anything said about him. But if a funeral sermon must be preached, let it be from these words: "Have mercy upon me, O God, according to Your lovingkindness; according to the multitude of Your tender mercies, blot out my transgressions."' In the same spirit of humility, he directed in his will that the following inscription and nothing more should be cut on his gravestone:

WILLIAM CAREY, BORN AUGUST 17, 1761
DIED …
A wretched, poor, and helpless worm
On Thy kind arms I fall.[2]

Great God of wonders, all Thy ways
  Are matchless, godlike, and divine;
But the fair glories of Thy grace
  More godlike and unrivalled shine:

Such dire offences to forgive,
  Such guilty daring souls to spare;
This is Thy grand prerogative,
  And none shall in the honour share:

---

2. Quoted by C.H. Spurgeon, *Morning and Evening*, edited by Roy H. Clarke (Thomas Nelson, 1994), August 29, morning.

In wonder lost, with trembling joy,
  We take the pardon of our God,
Pardon for sins of deepest dye,
  A pardon sealed with Jesus' blood:

O may this glorious matchless love,
  This God-like miracle of grace,
Teach mortal tongues, like those above,
  To raise this song of lofty praise:

Who is a pardoning God like Thee?
  Or who has grace so rich and free?

                    (Samuel Davies, 1723-61)

12

THE FAITHFULNESS OF GOD

We are looking at the attributes (or the essential qualities) that are intrinsic to God's moral character. That is to say, we are not looking at personality traits like congeniality or a sense of humour which are amoral. Even criminals (especially con-men) can have pleasant personalities. Rather, we are looking at what makes God, God. We are studying moral qualities that together constitute God's infinite and perfect goodness. So far we have looked at His holiness, love, mercy and grace. In this chapter we want to focus on God's faithfulness, by which we mean His loyalty to His people and the reliability of His promises. We live in a world where lying and prevaricating go all the way to the highest office; where marital infidelity is increasing all the time; where even in the church there are many who have taken ordination vows to abide by the articles of faith held by their denomination, and yet disregard them.

It is a great relief, then, to turn from the unfaithfulness on the part of men to 'the living and true God' who is absolutely faithful:

Therefore know that the LORD your God, He is God, the faithful God who keeps covenant and mercy for a thousand generations with those who love Him and keep His commandments (Deut. 7:9).

Your mercy, O LORD, is in the heavens; Your faithfulness reaches to the clouds (Ps. 36:5).

O LORD God of hosts, who is mighty like You, O LORD? Your faithfulness also surrounds You (Ps. 89:8).

Through the LORD's mercies we are not consumed, because His compassions fail not. They are new every morning; great is Your faithfulness (Lam. 3:22-23).

He who calls you is faithful, who also will do it (1 Thess. 5:24).

If we are faithless, He remains faithful; He cannot deny Himself (2 Tim. 2:13).

GOD'S FAITHFULNESS TO HIS ETERNAL COVENANT

The main way God portrays His faithfulness in the Bible (which is His self-revelation) is to present Himself as a *covenant-keeping* God. Twice in Nehemiah He is called the 'great and awesome God, You who keep Your covenant and mercy with those who love You and observe Your commandments' (Neh. 1:5; 9:32). Indeed, the religion of the Bible is covenant religion, and the Bible itself is made up of two sections called the Old Covenant (or Testament) and the New Covenant. Both Testaments record the history of 'the blood of the everlasting covenant' (Heb. 13:20) which began with Adam and Eve and the innocent animal blood shed in order for God to make 'tunics of skin' to cover the shame of their sin (Gen. 3:21-24). The word 'covenant' runs right through the Bible, occurring some three hundred times in the Old Testament, and some thirty times in the New Testament.

What then is a covenant? To quote Sinclair B. Ferguson: 'It refers to a promise confirmed by an oath of loyalty to the promise. When God makes His covenant with His people, He promises to be their God, and He binds Himself to that promise. As Hebrews 6:13-18 teaches us, when God made His covenant with Abraham, He staked His own existence on keeping it: He swore by Himself that He would fulfil it, because there was no one and nothing greater by which He could swear His oath! God's covenant is His marriage bond with His people. He commits Himself to us in unconditional love.'[1]

Consequently God's believing people are referred to in both Testaments as His wife or bride: '"For your Maker is your husband, the LORD of hosts is His name … for the LORD has called you like a woman forsaken and grieved in spirit, like a youthful wife when you were refused," says your God' (Isa. 54:5-6); and again, '"Let us be glad and rejoice and give Him glory, for the marriage of the Lamb has come, and His wife has made herself ready." And to her it was granted to be arrayed in fine linen, clean and bright, for the fine linen is the righteous acts of the saints' (Rev. 19:7-8; see also Jer. 3:14,20; 31:31-32; Hosea 2:19-20; 2 Cor. 11:2; Eph. 5:25; Rev. 21:1-2). Moreover, God's marriage vow to His bride is: 'I will take you as My people, and I will be your God' (Exod. 6:7); and again, 'And I heard a loud voice from heaven saying, "Behold, the tabernacle of God is with men, and He will dwell with them, and they shall be His people. God Himself will be with them and be their God"' (Rev. 21:3; see also Lev. 26:12; Jer. 24:7; Ezek. 37:23; Zech. 8:8; 2 Cor. 6:16). Altogether the divine vow is repeated eighteen times in Scripture.

---

1. Sinclair B. Ferguson, *A Heart for God*, pp. 58-59.

The purpose of God's everlasting covenant is, as it always was from the beginning, the gathering and sanctification of a countless multitude of redeemed people from 'all nations, tribes, peoples, and tongues' (Rev. 7:9), who will live with Him forever in a new heaven and a new earth in which righteousness dwells (2 Pet. 3:13; Rev. 21:1-4). God's covenant-making began with the fall of Adam and Eve into sin and His promise to provide a Saviour who would destroy the 'serpent' who had brought the curse of sin upon humanity (Gen. 3:15). Centuries later the divine covenant was reaffirmed with Noah (Gen. 6:17-18; 9:9-17), then Abraham (Gen. 12:1-3), then Moses (Exod. 2:24-25), and then David (2 Sam. 7:11-16; Ps. 89:1-4). Finally God Himself came in the Person of His Son, Jesus Christ (God incarnate), to fulfil all that was promised in the past by offering Himself as the only sacrifice whose blood was of sufficient worth to atone for the sin of the world (John 1:29; 1 John 4:10,14) and ratify His eternal covenant.

By that once-for-all sacrifice of Himself (Heb. 7:27; 9:26-28; 1 Pet. 3:18), Jesus Christ is able to bestow the covenant blessings of divine forgiveness, reconciliation and fellowship to all who come to God through Him (Matt. 26:28; Eph. 1:7; 2 Cor. 5:18; 1 John 1:3). As the writer of Hebrews explains, through the life, death, resurrection and exaltation of Jesus Christ, God's eternal covenant foreshadowed in the Old Testament is now perfectly fulfilled. As a result, Christ is now the 'Mediator of a better covenant, which was established on better promises' (Heb. 8:6), guaranteeing a better homeland, 'that is, a heavenly country' (Heb. 11:14-16). What a wonderful blessing to be living under the final and perfect terms of God's everlasting covenant with penitent, believing sinners. To quote J.I. Packer: 'The fulfilment of the old covenant in Christ opens the door of faith to the Gentiles. The "seed of Abraham," the defined community with which the covenant was made, was redefined in Christ. Gentiles with Jews who are united to Christ by faith become Abraham's seed in him (Gal. 3:26-29), while no one outside of Christ can be in covenant with God (Rom. 4:9-17; 11:13-24).'[2]

GOD HIMSELF IS THE MAKER AND KEEPER OF THE ETERNAL COVENANT

God's dealings with Abraham are a good illustration of God's power to make and keep covenant with His people. As the sovereign, almighty God, He does not negotiate the terms of the agreement with them, but unilaterally lays down the claims, promises and obligations that bind each party to the other in an eternal relationship: 'I will be your God, and you shall be My people.' Thus Genesis 12 tells us that God called Abraham out of idolatry in the city of Ur which belonged to the Chaldeans, saying: 'Now the LORD had said to Abram: "Get out of your country, from your family and from your father's house, to a land that I will show you. I will make you a great nation; I will bless you and make your name great; and you shall be a blessing. I will bless those who bless you, and I will curse him who curses you; and in you all the families of the earth shall be blessed." So Abram departed as the LORD had spoken to him, and Lot went with him. And Abram was seventy-five years old when he departed from Haran' (vv. 1-4).

After several years living childless in Canaan as a nomad, Abraham says to God in Genesis 15:3, 'Look, You have given me no offspring.' So to reassure Abraham, God commanded him to look at the night

---

2. J.I. Packer, *Concise Theology*, p. 89.

sky, saying, '"Count the stars if you are able to number them." And He said to him, "So shall your descendants be." And he believed in the LORD, and He accounted it to him for righteousness. Then He said to him, "I am the LORD, who brought you out of Ur of the Chaldeans, to give you this land to inherit it." And he said, "LORD God, how shall I know that I will inherit it?"' (Gen. 15:5-8). Abraham was not disputing God's word, but simply asking for some further confirmation of the promise God had originally given him. When even the best of men fail to keep their word, it was not easy for a new believer like Abraham to be absolutely convinced that God would be faithful and keep His promises against all odds. God therefore ratified His covenant with Abraham in the way people solemnly ratified important covenants with each other in those days (Gen. 15:9-16). He told Abraham to kill a one-year-old heifer, a three-year-old female goat and a three-year-old ram, and then cut them down the middle into two separate parts. Abraham was then to place each half of the animal opposite the other half in two straight rows, one below the other, on the ground. The two parties making the covenant would then walk between the two halves of the carcasses to signify that the penalty for breaking the covenant would be death. To 'make' a covenant was literally termed in Hebrew 'to cut' a covenant.

However, in this covenant only God passed between those pieces: 'And it came to pass, when the sun went down and it was dark, that behold, there appeared a smoking oven and a burning torch that passed between those pieces. On the same day the LORD made a covenant with Abram, saying: "To your descendants I have given this land, from the river of Egypt to the great river, the River Euphrates"' (vv. 17-18). The smoking oven and the burning torch were a symbol of God's presence. It was an awesome vision, and Abraham got the message. He could rely on God's covenant because of the ritual of the 'cutting'. As Sinclair B. Ferguson explains:

> God was saying, 'May I be cut off, like this, if My covenant is not fulfilled.' Little did Abraham know how great would be the cost to God of keeping this promise: He would be 'cut off from the land of the living; for the transgression of My people, He was stricken' (Isaiah 53:8), in order that those who were 'cut off' because of their sin, and were under God's curse, might receive the blessing promised to Abraham. God was, and is, faithful to His covenant. But more, He is faithful to His promise even to death – His Son's death – in order to bring blessing and salvation to His people.[3]

Abraham did not walk between the divided carcasses because God alone drew up the covenant, unilaterally imposed it, and was the party responsible for the fulfilment of the terms of this covenant. Abraham was going to be the *beneficiary*, but not the *benefactor*. Now this is important because the blessings promised were things that only God Himself could perform. God promised Abraham a son through whom he would become the father of 'a great nation', but Abraham was now over eighty years old and his wife over seventy and barren. To accentuate the problem God made them wait until Abraham was ninety-nine years old and Sarah ninety. There was no human possibility of her bearing a child. Again, because of a great famine, Abraham's grandson and great-grandsons will have to live in Egypt to avoid dying of starvation. And while they are living there they are going to be held captive

---

3. Sinclair B. Ferguson, ibid. pp. 63-64.

as slaves: 'Know certainly that your descendants will be strangers in a land that is not theirs, and will serve them, and they will afflict them four hundred years' (v. 13). God alone could rescue them and help them possess the land of Canaan: 'And also the nation whom they serve I will judge; and afterward they shall come out with great possessions. Now as for you, you shall go to your fathers in peace; you shall be buried at a good old age. But in the fourth generation they shall return here, for the iniquity of the Amorites is not yet complete' (vv. 14-16).

Abraham has nothing to be anxious about. God will give him a safe passage to heaven, and some four hundred years later God will bring his descendants back to the promised land of Canaan. Only the eternal, omnipotent God could make and keep a covenant like that. So we read in Joshua 21, 'The LORD gave to Israel all the land of which He had sworn to give to their fathers, and they took possession of it and dwelt in it … Not a word failed of any good thing which the LORD had spoken to the house of Israel. All came to pass' (vv. 43,45). The one true God is a faithful God. He has never overlooked anything or forgotten anything that He has promised to do.

FELLOWSHIP WITH GOD IS AT THE HEART OF HIS COVENANT

In Genesis 15:1 God says, 'Do not be afraid, Abram, I am your shield, your exceeding great reward.' In committing Himself to His covenant people, God is committing all His love and mercy and wisdom and power to them. In Isaiah 54:10 God says, 'For the mountains shall depart and the hills be removed, but My kindness shall not depart from you, nor shall My covenant of peace be removed.' Seven hundred years later God is still the chief blessing of the covenant reaffirmed in the New Testament with the coming of Jesus Christ. For what we see in the manger at Bethlehem in swaddling cloths is 'Emmanuel, which is translated, "God with us"' (Matt. 1:23). The angel also told Joseph to 'call His name Jesus' (v. 21, which means 'Jehovah is salvation'). So when we hear the teaching of Jesus and see Him dying on the cross to pay the debt of our sins and procure our salvation, it is God fulfilling His covenant to make Abraham a great nation, to give him a land, and through him to bring blessing to all people.

All three promises find their true and lasting fulfilment only in God our Saviour, Jesus Christ. Although God's covenant with Abraham was initially couched in material and earthly terms, its ultimate fulfilment was always intended to be *spiritual* and *heavenly*. This greater and deeper fulfilment of God's covenant with Abraham is what the gospel of Jesus Christ is all about. The word *gospel* means 'good news', and the good news is that through Jesus Christ (who is Abraham's seed, Gal. 3:29), God will create a spiritual posterity more numerous than the stars in the sky (Rev. 7:9), for Abraham is going to be 'the father of all those who believe' (Rom. 4:11). At no time has the Jewish nation been a numerous people (Deut. 7:7). The fulfilment of the 'land' God promised Abraham and his spiritual posterity is made clear in Hebrews 11. Canaan was just a shadow of something 'better, that is, a heavenly country. Therefore God is not ashamed to be called their God, for He has prepared a city for them' (v. 16).

The third promise, 'in you all the families of the earth shall be blessed' (Gen. 12:3) also has a spiritual fulfilment. The Jews have never brought material prosperity to all humankind. The blessings promised were the blessings of salvation; namely, reconciliation and fellowship with God forever. These were the blessings Jesus came to live and die to bring. As Paul says in Galatians 3:13-14, 'Christ has redeemed us from the curse of the law, having become a curse for us (for it is written, Cursed is everyone who hangs on a tree), that the blessing of Abraham might come upon the Gentiles in Christ Jesus, that we might receive the promise of the Spirit through faith.' The blessing of the Holy Spirit is the blessing of God Himself indwelling us as individuals and as a covenant community (1 Cor. 6:19-20; 3:16-17). That is the gospel: it is the good news that in Jesus Christ (God incarnate) all the blessings of God's covenant with Abraham are realised and enjoyed. And in a faint way, even Abraham himself had some understanding of the spiritual terms of the eternal covenant. For our Lord Jesus could say, 'Abraham rejoiced to see My day, and he saw it and was glad' (John 8:56). Abraham's faith was in Jesus Christ as the One through whom God would fulfil the covenant He had made with him. Thus Paul says, 'And the Scripture, foreseeing that God would justify the Gentiles by faith, preached the gospel to Abraham beforehand, saying, "In you all the nations shall be blessed" … Now to Abraham and his Seed were the promises made. He does not say, "And to seeds," as of many, but as of one, "And to your Seed," who is Christ' (Gal. 3:8,16).

THE COVENANT PROMISES ARE FOR BELIEVERS ONLY

In Genesis 15, when God reaffirms His covenant with Abraham, we read in verse 6 that 'he believed in the LORD.' He believed that God would bring blessing to all nations through his 'Seed'. God sought to create faith in Abraham by this solemn, binding agreement, and the fact that it did create faith, highlighted the great difference between Abraham and the other people in the city of Ur who worshipped idols and material prosperity. Abraham, however, believed in God as His supreme blessing. He built altars to the Lord and 'called on the name of the LORD' for help (Gen. 12:7-8). When Abraham defeated the enemies of the king of Sodom, the king in his gratitude offered Abraham all the captured booty as a reward. He assumed that Abraham was like everyone else in the world and wanted to get as rich as he could. But to his amazement Abraham declined his offer, saying, 'I will not take anything that is yours, lest you should say, "I have made Abram rich" ... After these things the word of the LORD came to Abram in a vision, saying, "Do not be afraid, Abram. I am your shield, your exceedingly great reward"' (Gen. 14:23; 15:1).

The promises of God meant more to Abraham than any riches to be gained from the world. Faith in the faithfulness of God to keep His promises divides believers from unbelievers. To the unbeliever the promises of the Bible are just words. They are not worth the paper they are written on, and so they dismiss them. They fail to understand that they are the words of One who does what He says, because He is 'the Possessor of heaven and earth' (Gen. 14:22). Thus David could say, 'For a day in Your courts is better than a thousand. I would rather be a doorkeeper in the house of my God than dwell in the tents of wickedness' (Ps. 84:10). David would gladly settle for such a menial position because God is a glorious and absolutely reliable promise-keeper. 'For,' he adds, 'the LORD God is a sun and shield; the LORD will give grace and glory; no good thing will He withhold from those who walk uprightly' (v. 11).

To a true believer, the promises of God are worth more than anything the world has to offer. Take the promises of God's covenant of grace signified in baptism and the Lord's Supper. What does an unbeliever see in these ordinances? Nothing of importance or value! They are just meaningless religious rituals! But that is not how a Christian thinks! He receives Christian baptism and the Lord's Supper as Abraham received circumcision; as a 'sign' and 'a seal of the righteousness of the faith' (Rom. 4:11). He or she hears God saying in these ordinances: 'Because you are united by faith to My Son, Jesus Christ in His death and resurrection, I have washed away all your sins in His blood and raised you to everlasting life by His Spirit' (Matt. 26:28; John 6:54; Eph. 1:7; Rom. 6:3-5). Baptism and the Lord's Supper are very precious and meaningful to a believer, because they strengthen our confidence in God's faithfulness to deliver on His promises. As Paul reasons in Romans 8:31-34, 'What then shall we say to these things? If God is for us, who can be against us? He who did not spare His own Son, but delivered Him up for us all, how shall He not with Him also freely give us all things? Who shall bring a charge against God's elect? It is God who justifies. Who is he who condemns? It is Christ who died, and furthermore is also risen, who is even at the right hand of God, who also makes intercession for us.' If God performed the greatest of all acts in giving His only Son to die for our sin, the apostle argues, can we not trust Him to perform the lesser act of bringing His redeemed people to glory? Of course he can! Both acts of redemption are included in God's covenant of grace (Gen. 3:15; Isa. 53:4-6; John 6:39; 10:27-30; Phil. 1:6).

In whom are we trusting for everlasting life and happiness with God in heaven? There are only two alternatives. We are either trusting in man (which could mean ourselves or some other human being who claims he can help us) or we are trusting God. If we are trusting in man, we are trusting in a lost cause, for all men are born sinners and are 'condemned already' (Ps. 51:5; John 3:18). Jesus Christ is the only Saviour God has provided for sinners, if they will put their trust in Him. 1 John 1:7-9 says, 'The blood of Jesus Christ His Son cleanses us from all sin ... if we confess our sins, He is faithful and just to forgive our sins and cleanse us from all unrighteousness.' Even in times of severe temptation we can have peace because 'God is faithful, who will not allow you to be tempted beyond what you are able, but with the temptation will also make the way of escape, that you may be able to bear it' (1 Cor. 10:13). That is God's promise, and every believer can count on it. Or if we fear that we may not be able to persevere to the end, God's word says, 'Now may the God of peace Himself sanctify you completely; and may your whole spirit, soul, and body be preserved blameless at the coming of our Lord Jesus Christ. He who calls you is faithful, who also will do it' (1 Thess. 5:23-24). The Christian lives and dies in that assurance. 'Let us hold fast the confession of our hope without wavering, for He who promised is faithful' (Heb. 10:23). No believer has ever been put to shame trusting in the faithfulness of God.

Hebrews 6:18 says, 'It is impossible for God to lie.' He will always do what He has said. He will never prove unfaithful to those who trust His word. Thus faith in Scripture is taking God at His word and relying on Him to fulfil what He has promised. For 'God is not a man, that He should lie, nor a son of man, that He should repent. Has He said, and will He not do? Or has He spoken, and will He not make it good?' (Num. 23:19).

Tell of His wondrous faithfulness,
And sound His power abroad;
Sing the sweet promise of His grace,
And our performing God.

Engraved as in eternal brass
The mighty promise shines;
Nor can the powers of darkness 'rase
Those everlasting lines.

His very word of grace is strong
As that which built the skies;
The voice that rolls the stars along
Speaks all the promises.

How would my leaping heart rejoice,
And think my heav'n secure!
I trust the all-creating voice,
And faith desires no more.

(Isaac Watts, 1674-1748)

13

THE JEALOUSY OF GOD

Jealousy is an attribute that seems unthinkable and even repulsive when associated with God, for jealousy can be regarded as one of the vilest sins among men: a loathsome spirit that leads to cruelty and vengeance. How could anyone imagine that the ugly trait of jealousy could be attributed to the God of the Bible who is absolutely holy and perfectly good? Is not jealousy clearly condemned in Scripture? In the Song of Solomon we read, 'Love is as strong as death; jealousy as cruel as the grave ... a most vehement flame' (8:6). Again, in Proverbs 27:4 God says, 'Wrath is cruel, and anger a torrent, but who is able to stand before jealousy?' The apostle Paul lists 'jealousies' among the works of the flesh in Galatians 5:20, and the apostle James says, 'For where jealousy and selfish ambition exist, there will be disorder and every vile practice' (James 6:16, ESV). How then can jealousy be attributed to God?

THE BIBLE AFFIRMS THAT GOD IS A JEALOUS GOD

It is very important to understand that when we seek to know who God is and what He is like, we do not rely on our own feelings or wisdom or imagination. Rather, we seek to listen to the words of Scripture where God has revealed all the truth about Himself that we need to know Him personally. God our Creator is infinitely above and beyond anything we could possibly imagine (Isa. 55:8-9). In His mercy, however, God has graciously revealed Himself to us through His prophets and apostles. Not only did God speak through them, but He had them put His words down in written form as a permanent record for all future generations. Certainly it is in the written word of God that we find the Holy Spirit speaking frequently of the jealousy of God. Jealousy is attributed to God twenty-five times in the Old Testament and at least twice in the New Testament. Here are some unambiguous references:

> You shall not make for yourself a carved image ... for I, the LORD your God, am a jealous God (Exod. 20:4-5).

> You shall worship no other God, for the LORD whose name is jealous, is a jealous God (Exod. 34:14).

> For the LORD your God is a consuming fire, a jealous God (Deut. 4:24).

> They have provoked Me to jealousy by what is not God; they have moved Me to anger by their foolish idols (Deut. 32:21).

> For they provoked Him to anger with their high places, and moved Him to jealousy with their carved images (Ps. 78:58).

Among other references, see also Deuteronomy 6:15; Joshua 24:19; 1 Kings 14:22; Ezekiel 8:3; Nahum 1:2; Zephaniah 1:18; 1 Corinthians 10:22; James 4:5. These Scriptures overwhelmingly show how jealousy, which is often denounced as a sin in man, is boldly ascribed as a *virtue* in God. How, then, can we reconcile these two things?

THE NATURE OF LAWFUL AND RIGHTEOUS JEALOUSY

Basically, to be jealous is to be resentful and intolerant of a known or suspected rival. It is an unwillingness to let someone else have what we consider is due to us. And, of course, whether our jealousy is right or wrong, is going to depend on whether the object of its focus lawfully belongs to us or not. If it does not, our jealousy is wrong. If it does, our jealousy is right. That is the all-important question: do I have a rightful claim to the object? So, for example, if we see others being admired for their success or gifts and resent it, we are sinning. For the admiration is due to them and not to us. Again, if we see a friend of ours making friends with others when we want to monopolise their friendship, we are desiring for ourselves what is not ours by right.

If, on the other hand, a husband sees his wife transferring her affections to a third party, he is right to be jealous, not with malice or vindictiveness, but to resent the intrusion of a rival for his wife's affections. For a husband and wife have made a covenant to love each other exclusively until death parts them. They have vowed to forsake all other suitors. They belong to each other, and have an exclusive right to each other's love as husband and wife. To see the affection of their spouse diverted to another lover is a just cause for jealousy. Indeed, the Old Testament recognised this sort of jealousy as a positive virtue by prescribing what Numbers 5:11-31 calls a 'jealous offering.' By this procedure a husband who suspected his wife of adultery could bring her before the Lord, and a priest would put her under oath. She was then required to drink bitter water which, if she had lied under oath before the Lord, would bring the curse of God upon her. It is one of the few examples in Scripture where human jealousy is regarded as normal and right, because it is proof that a man values his marriage as he should. Needless to say, the Bible consistently regards God's jealousy as being of this sort.

GOD'S JEALOUSY IS HOLY BECAUSE HE ALONE IS GOD

He demands the exclusive worship of all human beings because He is our Creator and there is no other God besides Him. How can people worship and serve substitute gods, as the devotees of all false religions do? There are no other gods to whom men can rightfully give their allegiance. This is explicitly stated in the first of the Ten Commandments: 'You shall have no other gods before Me' (Exod. 20:3). After that, it is repeated again and again throughout all the books of the Bible, but nowhere is it stated more clearly than in the prophecy of Isaiah: 'I am the LORD, and there is no other; there is no God besides Me' (Isa. 45:5), and again, 'I am the LORD, that is My name; and My glory I will not give to another, nor My praise to carved images' (Isa. 42:8).

God, however, is not only owed the exclusive worship of all His creatures, human and angelic, He also has in a special way the exclusive right to the worship of His covenant and redeemed people. God made a covenant with Abraham to be His God and to make him and his offspring God's people (Gen. 12:1-3; 15:1). That covenant was renewed with the children of Israel as God prepared to redeem them from slavery in Egypt: 'I will take you as My people, and I will be your God' (Exod. 6:7). It was solemnly ratified by the blood of sacrifice at Sinai and the same words used: 'I will walk among you and be your God and you shall be My people' (Lev. 26:12). This promise occurs many times in Scripture until finally the redeemed are in heaven and the apostle John says, 'Then I, John, saw the holy city, New Jerusalem, coming down out of heaven from God, prepared as a bride adorned for her husband. And I heard a loud voice from heaven saying: "Behold, the tabernacle of God is with men, and He will dwell with them, and they shall be His people, and God Himself will be with them and be their God"' (Rev. 21:2-3).

It is especially in the light of this repeated covenant that the Ten Commandments are intelligible. They are the rules governing the relationship between God and His covenant people. In them God is described five times as 'the LORD your God'. Moreover, this covenant is frequently portrayed in the Old Testament as a marriage covenant in which God is the heavenly bridegroom who has betrothed Israel to Himself as His bride. In Isaiah 54:5-6 God says to His people, 'For your Maker is your husband, the LORD of hosts is His name; and your Redeemer is the Holy One of Israel; He is called the God of the whole earth. For the LORD has called you like a woman forsaken and grieved in spirit, like a youthful wife when you were refused, says your God.' And because He had set His love on Israel, He naturally expected His people to faithfully love and serve Him. He demanded their undivided attention and loyalty. The worship of idols, therefore, constituted a breach of the marriage covenant that God saw as spiritual adultery, provoking Him to jealousy and anger.

Thus of Israel it is said that when Israel 'grew fat ... then he forsook God who made him, and scornfully esteemed the Rock of his salvation. They provoked Him to jealousy with foreign gods; with abominations they provoked Him to anger' (Deut. 32:15-16). In Ezekiel 8:3 an idol worshipped in Jerusalem is called 'the image of jealousy which provokes to jealousy'; and in Ezekiel 16:38 God depicts Israel as His adulterous wife who is engaging in unholy associations with idols and idolaters in Canaan: 'I will judge you as women who break wedlock or shed blood are judged. I will bring blood upon you in fury and jealousy.' This is what God means when He says that His 'name is jealous' and that He is a 'jealous God'. He has made an eternal covenant with His chosen, believing people that requires a reciprocal love and loyalty.

THE IMPLICATIONS OF THE JEALOUSY OF GOD

Quite simply, they are twofold. The first is that:

God's jealousy demands our undivided love
The Ten Commandments are divine requirements laid down for all human beings by their Creator. The first two, in order of priority, prohibit the worship of anything, material or immaterial, except the living and true God, who brooks no rivals. The worship of substitute gods or graven images is an offence against our Creator's rightful claim over our lives. It is spiritual rebellion and insubordination of the highest order deserving of death as the law of God requires (Ezek. 18:20; Rom. 6:23). When professing Christians worship substitute gods by loving pleasure, possessions, power, family or anything else more than God, it is a double offence. It is to be guilty, not only of spiritual insubordination, but also spiritual infidelity. God is both our Maker and our Husband (Isa. 54:5-6).

Thus James 4:4 says, 'Adulterers and adulteresses! Do you not know that friendship with the world is enmity with God? Whoever therefore wants to be a friend of the world makes himself an enemy of God.' James, of course, is speaking metaphorically of the spiritual marriage between God and His people. He is accusing some of his Christian readers of unfaithfulness to God or spiritual adultery. The same charge is made against Israel in Jeremiah 3:14,20: '"Return, O backsliding children," says the LORD, "for I am married to you … surely as a wife treacherously departs from her husband, so have you dealt treacherously with Me, O house of Israel," says the LORD.' Likewise, Paul says in 2 Corinthians 11:2, 'I am jealous for you with a godly jealousy. For I have betrothed you to one husband, that I may present you as a chaste virgin to Christ.'

Jesus Christ came down from heaven to seek for Himself a bride, the Christian church (Matt. 25:1-13; Rev. 19:7-9; 21:2,9-11). He has purchased us with the priceless dowry of His own precious blood, God's blood (Acts 20:28), and made an everlasting covenant with us. We are no longer our own. We belong to Christ exclusively (1 Cor. 6:19-20). So to court the world's friendship, says James, is to commit spiritual adultery and arouse the 'enmity' of God. The apostle continues: 'Or do you think that the Scripture says in vain ['to no purpose', ESV] "the Spirit who dwells in us yearns jealously"?' (James 4:4-5). The Spirit of whom James speaks here is the Holy Spirit. And the Holy Spirit whom God has made to dwell in us (1 Cor. 6:19) will not share living quarters with the world and all its corrupting enticements. We are His, and He 'yearns jealously' to have all of us.

Now we could be tempted to argue that we are not going after other gods. We read our Bible and pray and go to church regularly. That may be so! But it could also be mere lip-service (an outward formality). We may be no better than Israel who 'feared the LORD, yet served their own gods – according to the ritual of the nations from among whom they were carried away' (2 Kings 17:33). It is not necessary to bow before a 'graven image' to commit idolatry. Worldliness and covetousness are also forms of idolatry (Col. 3:5). James says the same thing in chapter 4:2, 'You lust and do not have. You murder and covet and cannot obtain. You fight and war [or quarrel, ESV]. Yet you do not have because you do not ask. You ask and do not receive, because you ask amiss, that you may spend it on your pleasures. Adulterers and adulteresses!'

It is a picture of utter self-centredness, and such obsession with our own pleasure is worldliness because it makes a god out of the world's fleeting pleasures and fading prizes. These are the things a worldly professing Christian prays for, and although James does not say that God does not hear those prayers, he does say, 'You ask and do not receive because you ask amiss, that you may spend it on your pleasures.' God always hears our prayers, but sometimes the answer has to be 'no' because our motives are selfish and sinful. God's promise is to supply our need, not our greed. 'Pure and undefiled religion before God and the Father is this: to visit orphans and widows in their trouble, and to keep oneself unspotted from the world' (James 1:27).

It would seem that this is by and large the state of the church in the West today. The institutional church is generally-speaking a worldly church. People may attend a Christian worship service on a Sunday, but during the rest of the week there is no apparent difference between their lifestyle and that of those who are not Christians. Their conversation, thoughts and interests; the books they read and the friends they prefer; the way they spend their time and money, are all evidence of their love for the world, rather than

God. They are spiritual adulterers and adulteresses, and the Lord will not tolerate it. Jesus said, 'No one can serve two masters; for either he will hate the one and love the other, or else he will be loyal to the one and despise the other. You cannot serve God and mammon' (Matt. 6:24). God jealously yearns for our undivided love.

Spurgeon has some moving words on the theme of 'Sacred Jealousy':

> Believer, your Lord is jealous of your love. Did He choose you? He cannot bear that you would choose another. Did He buy you with His own blood? He cannot endure that you would think you are your own, or that you belong to this world. He loved you with such a love that He would not stop in heaven without you. He would sooner die than you should perish. He cannot endure anything standing between your heart's love and Him … He is also jealous of our company. There should be no one with whom we converse so much as with Jesus. To abide in Him only, this is true love. To commune with the world, to find sufficient solace in our carnal comforts, this is grievous to our jealous Lord. He wants us to abide in Him and enjoy His constant fellowship. Many of the trials He sends are to wean our hearts from the creature and fix them more closely on Him. Let this jealousy, which should keep us near Christ, also comfort us. If He loves so much as to care about our love, we may be sure nothing will harm us, for He will protect us from all our enemies.[1]

God's jealousy requires our unflagging zeal

God's people should be positively and passionately devoted to His honour and His cause. The biblical word for this is *zeal* and it stems from godly jealousy.

---

1. C.H. Spurgeon, *Morning and Evening*, September 12, morning.

Just as God says in Zechariah 1:14, 'I am jealous for Jerusalem and for Zion with a great jealousy', so we should feel jealousy for Him and work for the glory of His name. Indeed, this is a very important test of the depth of our Christian lives. The great men of the Bible were commended for their jealousy and zeal for God. Elijah could say, 'I have been very zealous for the LORD God of hosts; for the children of Israel have forsaken Your covenant, torn down Your altars, and killed Your prophets with the sword. I alone am left; and they seek to take my life' (1 Kings 19:14). Again, when Phineas the priest speared the drunken Israelite who flaunted his Midianite prostitute after God had condemned the people for their harlotry with the women of Moab, he was commended by the Lord who said, 'Phineas ... has turned back My wrath from the children of Israel, because he was zealous with My zeal ... among them, so that I did not consume the children of Israel in My zeal' (Num. 25:11).

The apostle Paul also had such a zeal. He says to the Corinthians: 'I am jealous for you with godly jealousy. For I have betrothed you to one husband, that I may present you as a chaste virgin to Christ. But I fear, lest somehow, as the serpent deceived Eve by his craftiness, so your minds may be corrupted from a sincere and pure devotion to Christ.' But the greatest example of jealous zeal for God, of course, is our Lord Jesus who, when He saw the temple profaned by the evil trafficking of the merchants and money-changers, drove them out, saying: 'It is written, "My house shall be called a house of prayer, but you have made it a den of thieves"' (Matt. 21:13). According to John, it was then that 'His disciples remembered that it was written, "Zeal for Your house has eaten Me up"' (John 2:17). Godly jealousy is to zeal what cause is to effect. Jealousy for the honour of God and His house consumed Jesus. He was eaten up with it. In this matter of zeal for God, as in all other things, our Lord has left us an example to follow in His steps.

When we look upon the world today, as it gives its worship to things that are no gods, as we see our friends and neighbours drawn to false cults, do we feel no stirrings of divine jealousy within us? Do we feel no pain that the homage and allegiance that belongs to Christ is being given to utterly inferior objects? Or what about the moral drift in society with the legalising of abortion, pornography, same-sex marriage, gambling and the use of the Lord's Day for entertainment, rather than the worship of Almighty God? Do these things not break our hearts? Can we say with the Psalmist, 'Rivers of water run down from my eyes, because men do not keep Your law' (Ps. 119:136)? Or again, consider the backslidden state of many Christian churches where there is 'a famine ... of hearing the words of the Lord' (Amos 8:11), irregular attendance and unfaithful stewardship. If these things do not move us to action and to prayer, it is because we are not eaten up with zeal for God's name and God's house as Jesus was.

Our interest, time and energies are being spent on building our own kingdom instead of God's. We have no consuming passion for God's glory. This is a dangerous spiritual condition to be in, for our Lord would rather that we boil with indignation or freeze with indifference than insult Him with a complacency that nauseates. His message to us in our half-heartedness is His message to the church at Laodicea: 'Be zealous and repent!' If the Lord was prepared to spew the Laodicean church out of His mouth for their spiritual lukewarmness, He will surely not spare us if we fail to repent (Rev. 3:14-22).

Although Bishop J.C. Ryle's (1816-1900) definition of zeal for God is often quoted, it bears repetition because it is simple and searching, and no one has said it better, as of yet:

> A zealous man in religion is pre-eminently *a man of one thing*. It is not enough to say that he is earnest, hearty, uncompromising, thorough-going, whole-hearted, fervent in spirit. He only sees one thing, he cares for one thing, he lives for one thing ... He burns for one thing; and that one thing is to please God, and to advance God's glory. If he is consumed in the very burning, he cares not for it, – he is content. He feels that, like a lamp, he is made to burn; and if consumed in burning, he has but done the work for which God appointed him. Such an one will always find a sphere for his zeal. If he cannot preach, and work, and give money, he will cry, and sigh, and pray. Yes: if he is only a pauper, on a perpetual bed of sickness, he will make the wheels of sin around him drive heavily, by continually interceding against it. If he cannot fight in the valley with Joshua, he will do the work of Moses, Aaron, and Hur, on the hill (Exod. xvii. 9-13). If he is cut off from working himself, he will give the Lord no rest till help is raised up from another quarter, and the work is done. This is what I mean when I speak of 'zeal' in religion.[2]

Zeal or single-minded devotion to the living and true God, and to His only Son, Jesus Christ our Lord, is a virtue to be much desired and pursued, but it must be in accordance with the will of God. Concerning the unbelieving Jews of his day, Paul says, 'I bear them witness that they have a zeal for God but not according to knowledge' (Rom. 10:2). They were clinging to the old covenant of animal sacrifices, instead of trusting

---

2. J.C. Ryle, *Practical Religion* (James Clarke, 1970), p. 130.

in Christ's once-for-all sacrifice of Himself for the sin of the world. As a result, they ignorantly persecuted the church. James and John wanting to call down fire from heaven upon a Samaritan village, and Peter cutting off the right ear of Malchus, the servant of the Jewish high priest, are also examples of zeal without knowledge (Luke 9:54; John 18:10). Such zeal is not glorifying to God.

A zeal according to knowledge is a zeal provoked by jealousy for the glory of God according to the will of God. And what is the will of God? First, the will of God is for our sanctification (1 Thess. 4:3). We glorify God by striving for holiness. Paul had this zeal: 'Brethren, I do not count myself to have apprehended; but one thing I do, forgetting those things which are behind and reaching forward to those things which are ahead, I press toward the goal for the prize of the upward call of God in Christ Jesus' (Phil. 3:13-14). Secondly, it is the will of God that we proclaim the truth and refute error: 'Beloved, while I was very diligent to write to you concerning our common salvation, I found it necessary to write to you exhorting you to contend earnestly for the faith which was once for all delivered to the saints' (Jude 3). Truth saves lives, heresy destroys them (John 8:32; Gal. 1:9). Thirdly, it is the will of God that we should 'Go into all the world and preach the gospel to every creature. He who believes and is baptised will be saved; but he who does not believe will be condemned' (Mark 16:15-16; see also Matt. 28:18-20). God loves the world (John 3:16). He is 'not willing that any should perish, but that all should come to repentance' (2 Pet. 3:9). But for sinners to repent and believe in Christ, they must hear the gospel from those sent out to proclaim it to the ends of the earth (Acts 1:8; Rom. 10:14-15). Fourthly, it is

God's will that His people should be 'zealous for good works' (Titus 2:14): works of kindness, generosity, visitation, hospitality, encouragement, helpfulness and edification, to name a few (Matt. 5:13-16; 25:31-46).

In this time of rampant materialism and high living standards in the West, many Christian churches and individuals have become spiritually lukewarm like the church in Laodicea (Rev. 3:14-22). There is a dearth of believers who share God's jealousy for the glory of His name and the advancement of His kingdom on earth. Who is more worthy of our undivided love than Christ, the God-man, who purchased our salvation at the enormous cost of bearing in our place the just punishment which our sins deserve? And what is more worthy of our unflagging zeal than the glory of God and the salvation of souls for whom Jesus died? Nothing! It is better to work with the little we have, than not to work at all. If we only have one talent, let us not bury it in the ground (Luke 19:11-27). Let us live so as to be missed. Let us spend and be spent like Jesus who said, 'I must work the works of Him who sent Me while it is day; the night is coming when no one can work' (John 9:4). 'Therefore be zealous and repent' (Rev. 3:19).

14

THE WRATH OF GOD

The wrath of God may be defined as His intense righteous hatred of sin and everything that is opposed to His moral character; in particular, His holiness and justice. The Bible, therefore, in both the Old and New Testaments, reveals God as a God of wrath as well as a God of love. Some think He cannot be both, but it is an axiom of the Bible that there is no incompatibility between these two attributes of the divine nature. All God's attributes belong together like different pieces of a jigsaw puzzle. The whole picture of God's being and character is only seen when they are put together. God's love is a holy love. It cannot love what is impure or insubordinate. His wrath is a holy wrath. It cannot be unjust or capricious or uncontrolled.

A.W. Pink is helpful here:

Now the wrath of God is as much a Divine perfection as is His faithfulness, power, or mercy. It *must be* so, for there is no blemish whatever, not the slightest defect in the character of God; yet there *would be* if 'wrath' were absent from Him! Indifference to sin is a moral blemish, and he who hates it not is a moral leper. How could He who is the Sum of all excellence look with equal satisfaction upon virtue and vice, wisdom and folly? How could He who is infinitely holy disregard sin and refuse to manifest His 'severity' (Rom. 11:22) toward it? How could He, who delights only in that which is pure and lovely, not loathe and hate that which is impure and vile? The very nature of God makes Hell as real a necessity, as imperatively and eternally requisite, as Heaven is. Not only is there no imperfection in God, but there is no perfection in Him that is less perfect than another. The wrath of God is His eternal detestation of all unrighteousness. It is the displeasure and indignation of Divine equity against evil. It is the holiness of God stirred into activity against sin.[1]

Our problem is that we have such sentimental notions about the love of God that we find it difficult to imagine God ever being angry. And yet the attribute of wrath is a very important part of God's character. Without it there would be no need for some of God's other attributes. For if God cannot in any sense be angry with sinners, what do we mean when we say that He is being patient with them? If God is not subject to real and intense provocation by human sin, then to speak of the grace and mercy of God becomes meaningless. A God who is not provoked by wrong does not need to be gracious or longsuffering. His composure would merely reflect moral indifference or insensitivity. The Bible, therefore, is never embarrassed to assert that God is personally affronted by sin and personally executes judgment on sinners. We must never make the mistake of interpreting God's patience towards sinners as divine indifference to sin. We must never fall into the error of being complacent about

1. A.W. Pink, *The Attributes of God*, p. 83.

wrongdoing. Failure to meet God's moral standards provokes God intensely, and it is only because He is longsuffering that that provocation does not lead to our immediate destruction. It would be convenient if this were not so; if the idea of an angry God were a hangover from an outdated and primitive religion, but we cannot say that. There is a divine decree that condemns at death all impenitent sinners to everlasting hell.

Unfortunately, modern sentimentality has made inroads into the professing Christian community, and there has been widespread neglect and indeed denial of the doctrine of the wrath of God, in consequence of which the 'severity of God' (Rom. 11:22) has largely been lost sight of, with disastrous results in many spheres of life. Thus a theologian like J.I. Packer can write:

> The modern habit throughout the Christian church is to play this subject down. Those who still believe in the wrath of God (not all do) say little about it; perhaps they do not think much about it. To an age which has unashamedly sold itself to the gods of greed, pride, sex, and self-will, the Church mumbles on about God's kindness, but says virtually nothing about His judgment. How often during the past year did you hear, or if you are a minister, did you preach, a sermon on the wrath of God? How long is it, I wonder, since a Christian spoke straight on this subject on radio or television, or in one of those half-column sermonettes that appear in some national dailies and magazines? (And if a man did so, how long would it be before he would be asked to speak or write again?) The fact is that the subject of divine wrath has become taboo in modern society, and Christians by and large have accepted the taboo and conditioned themselves never to raise the matter.[2]

2. J.I. Packer, *Knowing God*, p. 134.

THE TESTIMONY OF SCRIPTURE TO GOD'S WRATH

The Bible clearly teaches that just as God is good to those who trust Him for salvation, so He is vengeful and full of fury to those who reject His salvation and remain impenitent in their sins. Scripture says:

> Now see that I, even I, am He, and there is no God besides Me; I kill and I make alive; I wound and I heal; nor is there any who can deliver from My hand. For I raise My hand to heaven, and say, 'As I live forever, if I whet My glittering sword, and My hand takes hold on judgment, I will render vengeance to My enemies, and repay those who hate Me' (Deut. 32:39-41).

> God is a just judge, and God is angry with the wicked every day (Ps. 7:11).

> The wicked shall be turned into hell, and all the nations that forget God (Ps. 9:17).

> God is jealous, and the LORD avenges; the LORD avenges and is furious. The LORD will take vengeance on His adversaries, and He reserves wrath for His enemies; the LORD is slow to anger and great in power, and will not at all acquit the wicked ... Who can stand before His indignation? And who can endure the fierceness of His anger? His fury is poured out like fire, and the rocks are thrown down by Him. The LORD is good, a stronghold in the day of trouble; and He knows those who trust in Him. But with an overflowing flood He will make an utter end of its place, and darkness will pursue His enemies (Nahum 1:2-8).

> ... when the Lord Jesus is revealed from heaven with His mighty angels, in flaming fire taking vengeance on those who do not know God, and on those who do not obey the gospel of our Lord Jesus Christ. These

shall be punished with everlasting destruction from the presence of the Lord and from the glory of His power, when He comes, in that Day, to be glorified in His saints and to be admired among all those who believe, because our testimony among you was believed (2 Thess. 1:7-10; see also Rom. 1:18; 2:5; 5:9; 12:19; Eph. 5:6; Col. 3:6; Heb. 3:11; Rev. 6:17; 19:15).

The whole Bible from Genesis to Revelation gives evidence of God's continuous anger toward sinners and His righteous judgment of them even in this life. It starts with the angels in heaven before the world was created. God cast Satan and the angels who rebelled with him out of heaven to await final and eternal hell (Matt. 8:29; Jude 6). In Genesis 3, no sooner has God created the world, when Satan entices Adam and Eve to rebel against Him too, and both of them are cursed with death and expelled from the Garden. Fifteen hundred years later, the world was so filled with wickedness and violence that God destroyed with a flood the entire race, save Noah and his family (Gen. 6–8). Five hundred years later God was again provoked to anger and destroyed by fire all the inhabitants of the twin cities of Sodom and Gomorrah because of their homosexuality (Gen. 18 and 19). Another six hundred years later, God killed every firstborn male in Egypt as well as Pharaoh's whole army, because He was angry with their cruel treatment of His people (Exod. 12:29-42; 14:1-31). At the beginning of the forty years of wandering in the wilderness of Sinai, when the Israelites made a golden calf and worshipped it, God destroyed 'about three thousand men' (Exod. 32:28). During the rest of the journey many more died because they provoked God to wrath by their sin. When they inherited the promised land of Canaan, God warned them many times that if they worshipped other gods they would be suppressed by their heathen neighbours. This happened repeatedly, as recorded in the book of Judges. Ultimately they were carried into captivity; first, when the ten tribes in the northern kingdom were carried into Assyria in 722 B.C. (2 Kings 17:6), and then about a hundred and forty years later when the two tribes of Judah were taken captive into Babylon (2 Kings 24:13-16).

Now critics of the biblical doctrine of divine wrath argue that all the above is simply the history of the religion of the Bible in its most primitive form. When you get to the religion of Jesus and the New Testament, they say, the idea of a God of wrath is replaced by a God of love. The truth, however, is to the contrary. For references to God's wrath and the final judgment occur in every book of the New Testament except Philemon. *The wrath of God* is referred to at least twenty-five times and the word *hell* comes eleven times (ten of them from the lips of Jesus), and references to divine vengeance or destruction or judgment scores of times.

Just before His crucifixion, Jesus Himself predicted the destruction of Jerusalem and its temple, because the Jewish nation had rejected Him as their Messiah (Matt. 24:1-2). Moreover, He could not have spoken more plainly than when He said: 'He who believes in the Son has everlasting life; and he who does not believe the Son shall not see life, but the wrath of God abides on Him'; and again, 'When the Son of Man comes in His glory, and all the holy angels with Him, then He will sit on the throne of His glory. All the nations will be gathered before Him, and He will separate them one from another, as a shepherd divides his sheep from the goats. And He will set the sheep on His right hand, but the goats on the left. Then the King will say to those on His right hand: "Come, you blessed of My Father, inherit the kingdom prepared for you from the foundation of the world" ... then He will also say to those on the left hand: "Depart from Me, you cursed, into the everlasting fire prepared for the devil and his angels"' (John 3:36; Matt. 25:31-41). In Revelation 6:15-16, John says that on the last day 'every slave and every free man hid themselves in the caves and in the rocks of the mountains, and said to the mountains and rocks, "Fall on us, and hide us from the face of Him who sits on the throne and from the wrath of the Lamb."'

The final event of history is without doubt unimaginable, but nevertheless real. The Bible is a book for realists. It treats us like adults, and refuses to comfort us with sentimental fairy stories ending on the note: 'And they all lived happily ever after.' To those who say, 'My God would never send anyone to hell', our reply must be: 'Of course he would not! Your god would never say boo to a goose! He is nothing but a spiritual teddy bear; a comfort toy, a fantasy that has no existence outside your own imagination. You are living in a fool's paradise.' To quote the theologian, R.C. Sproul, 'If God is holy at all, if God has an ounce of justice in His character, indeed if God exists as God, how could He possibly be anything else but angry with us? We violate His holiness, we insult His justice, we make light of His grace. These things can hardly be pleasing to Him ... But a God of love who has no wrath is no God. He is an idol of our own making, as much as if we carved Him out of stone.'[3]

The only reliable source of truth about God is Scripture. The Bible is the only book written by God about God. It is in a sense God's abbreviated autobiography. The Bible is about the real God, and

---

3. R.C. Sproul, *The Holiness of God* (Tyndale House, 1997), pp. 224,228.

not about a hypothetical deity. It reveals a God who cares fervently about His glory and His righteousness; a God who has already destroyed the world one time by water. Why should it be so unthinkable that He will destroy it and us again by fire as He has warned (2 Pet. 3:10)? Some may be embarrassed to accept such a thought, but not God. He is no more embarrassed about hell, than He is about the flood or Sodom or Gomorrah. God's wrath is not a subject that is taboo in heaven. Rather, God's wrath is prayed for and answered in heaven, because it punishes the evildoer and not the victim (Rev. 6:10-11). Supremely, it seeks the glory of God and the good of all His redeemed.

THE NATURE OF GOD'S WRATH

God's wrath is righteous anger and indignation. It is His moral outrage and intolerance of all rebellion and wrongdoing. God's anger is not like human anger which even at its best is tainted with selfishness, vindictiveness, irritability, folly and lack of control. It is also a mark of human anger that we vacillate and change our minds. We threaten to punish wrongdoing, but often fail to follow through. Or again, we punish one person less than another for the same sin. Or we punish someone who is absolutely innocent. All of us have been wrongly punished at some time. God's anger, however, is perfectly controlled by His holiness, His omniscience, His wisdom, His justice, His love and His omnipotence. These things exclude all uncertainty and caprice from the wrath of God. He does not inflict injury for the sake of it, or in return for injury received. For as A.W. Pink says, 'Though God will vindicate His dominion as Governor of the universe, He will not be vindictive.'[4] God is only angry when anger is righteously called for.

---

4. A.W. Pink, *ibid*, p. 83.

THE PURPOSE OF GOD'S WRATH IS RETRIBUTIVE

It is God rendering to men and women what they justly deserve which is what one should expect from 'the Judge of all the earth' (Gen. 18:25). To reward good with good, and evil with evil, is a Godlike trait, and being made in the image of God, our conscience tells us that this is right. That is how it ought to be. Retribution is a natural expression of the divine character. Retribution is an inescapable fact of God's moral being. A just and holy God cannot be morally indifferent or insensitive to sin and wrongdoing which violate the rights of God and others. So when the Bible speaks of the final judgment, it always portrays it in terms of retribution. Jesus says that He 'will come in the glory of His Father with His angels, and then He will reward each according to his works' (Matt. 16:27). Paul in Romans 2:5-11 speaks of '...the righteous judgment of God, who "will render to each one according to his deeds"; eternal life to those who by patient continuance in doing good seek for glory, honor, and immortality; but to those who are self-seeking and do not obey the truth, but obey unrighteousness—indignation and wrath, tribulation and anguish, on every soul of man who does evil, of the Jew first and also of the Greek; but glory, honor, and peace to everyone who works what is good, to the Jew first and also to the Greek. For there is no partiality with God.'

Even Christians will come under the retributive justice of God. Although all 'born again' Christians will go to heaven, those who have not faithfully served their Saviour on earth will not receive the same reward as those who have. Paul makes this clear in 1 Corinthians 3:8-15 when he says, 'Each one will receive his own reward according to his labour ... I have laid the foundation, and another builds on it. But let each one take heed how he builds on it ... Now if anyone builds on this foundation with gold, silver, precious stones, wood, hay, straw, each one's work will become clear; for the Day [of judgment] will declare it, because it will be revealed by fire; and the fire will test each one's work, of what sort it is. If anyone's work which he has built on it endures, he will receive a reward. If anyone's work is burned, he will suffer loss; but he himself will be saved, yet so as through fire.' For God to judge justly is His glory; and the final judgment will be His way of removing from all humanity the suspicion that He has ceased to care about right or wrong, and is partial to some. J.L. Dagg, the nineteenth-century American theologian, has this reply: 'Every one will be brought to judgment as if he were the only creature present, and every one will give an account of himself, and receive sentence for himself with as much discrimination and perfection of justice as if the judge were wholly absorbed in the consideration of his single cause.'[5]

THE WAY OF ESCAPE FROM GOD'S WRATH

God's wrath in the Bible is ultimately something that men choose for themselves. It is a destiny perfectly suited to the godless life they love so much and refuse to give up. Hell is not an arbitrary infliction of God's wrath. It is deserved, because the impenitent shun God all their lives, preferring to serve and please themselves rather than love and serve Him. Thus in the end God gives them what they want, nothing more and nothing less. Nobody stands under the wrath of God save those who have resolutely chosen to reject God, come what may.

---

5. J.L. Dagg, *Manual of Theology and Church Order* (Gano Books, n.d.), p. 356.

God's readiness to respect human choice may seem strange, for 'God our Saviour desires all men to be saved and to come to the knowledge of the truth' (1 Tim. 2:3-4). Moreover, at infinite cost to Himself, God has provided a way for sinners to escape His wrath through the death of His Son on the cross as an atoning sacrifice. The impenitent, however, will have none of God's loving overtures. They 'suppress the truth in unrighteousness, because what may be known of God is manifest in them, for God has shown it to them' (Rom. 1:18-19). Accordingly, Paul asks, 'Do you think ... that you will escape the judgment of God? Or do you despise the riches of His goodness, forbearance and longsuffering, not knowing that the goodness of God leads you to repentance? But in accordance with your hardness and your impenitent heart you are storing up for yourself wrath in the day of wrath' (Rom. 2:3-5).

God is patient, but His patience cannot extend beyond our death. The fact that God in His goodness allows us to go on enjoying health and good fortune even when we persistently reject His salvation, does not mean that we are safe. He is being 'longsuffering towards us', says Peter, 'not willing that any should perish, but that all should come to repentance' (2 Pet. 3:9). If we are still alive, it is only for one reason: God is holding back His wrath in order to provide us with more opportunity to repent and be saved. But if our response to His goodness and patience is simply to become more set in our godlessness, we have to beware. For there is all the difference in the world between being granted probation by the judge and getting away with the crime. When God sends impenitent sinners to hell, they truly deserve it. As Paul says in Romans 1:29-32, 'who knowing the righteous judgment of God, that those who practise such things [such things as 'unrighteousness, sexual immorality, wickedness, covetousness ... deceit ... disobedience to parents', to name a few] are deserving of death, not only do the same, but also approve of those who practise them.' It is a death wish, like whales who beach themselves, or lemmings who rush in great numbers over a precipice to certain death. Each step impenitent sinners take away from God is a conscious, voluntary move in the direction of hell, and if we keep insisting that we do not want God interfering in our lives, in the end He will grant our wish. He will withdraw His mercy from us forever. Impenitence is the only sin God cannot forgive, because no pardon is desired.

God will punish our impenitence just as certainly as He punished every impenitent sinner in Noah's day. There are only two places in the universe where God can punish sin. One is in hell where men and women experience forever the wrath of God against their persistent moral perversity and hardness. The other place is the cross, where Jesus (God incarnate) bore in His own Person, in one horrific stroke of divine justice, that same wrath on our behalf. Calvary is the only place where we can escape from God's wrath. For there, in amazing love, Christ bore the punishment that our sins justly deserve. Both Paul and John call His death a propitiatory sacrifice (Rom. 3:25; 1 John 2:2; 4:10). To propitiate is to appease the wrath of God. This is the heart of the gospel: that Jesus Christ, by virtue of His death on the cross as our substitute and sin-bearer has turned away God's wrath from us by letting it fall on Himself. 'For Christ also suffered once for sins, the just for the unjust, that He might bring us to God, being put to death in the flesh but made alive by the Spirit' (1 Pet. 3:18). The choice is ours: the eternal torment of hell because we despise the goodness of God that leads to repentance; or the unending bliss of heaven because we take by faith the death of Christ on the cross as the only way of escape 'from the wrath to come' (1 Thess. 1:10).

15

THE GLORY OF GOD

The glory of God is the main theme of the Bible. There are literally hundreds of references to His glory. In Stephen's defence against the charge of blasphemy by the Jewish priests, he begins with the words: 'The God of glory appeared to our father Abraham', and it ends with the words: 'But he being full of the Holy Spirit, gazed into heaven and saw the glory of God, and Jesus standing at the right hand of God' (Acts 7:2,55). The living and true God is a 'God of glory'. The Scriptures speak of 'the glory of God the Father' (Phil. 2:11), 'the glory as of the only begotten [Son] of the Father, full of grace and truth' (John 1:14, 3:16); and 'the Spirit of glory and of God' (1 Pet. 4:14). Accordingly, the first question in the Westminster Shorter Catechism is: 'What is the chief end of man?' And the answer is: 'Man's chief end is to glorify God and to enjoy Him for ever.'

THE GLORY OF GOD DEFINED

The glory of God is spoken of in the Scriptures in a twofold sense. In the first place, there is the glory that is *intrinsic and essential* to His divine being and character.

This is what God is in Himself as the Supreme Being. It is the excellence and splendour of the sum total of all His attributes which are eternally and infinitely perfect. 'God is Spirit' and therefore invisible to the naked human eye, unless God visibly manifests His glory to us (John 4:24, cf. 1:14-18). But whether He manifests it or not, God's glory is as essential to His being as light is to the burning mass of the sun, whether it is hidden by clouds or not. God was answering Moses' plea to be shown God's glory when He proclaimed to Moses His name (i.e. the perfection of His character and power, Exod. 33:18-34:7). With that proclamation, however, went an awe-inspiring physical manifestation of what is called the Shekinah, a bright shining cloud that could look like fire (Exod. 24:15-17). The Shekinah was itself called the glory of God and it appeared at various times in biblical history (Exod. 40:34-35; cf. Lev. 9:23-24; 1 Kings 8:10-11; Ezek. 1:28; 10:4; Matt. 17:5; Luke 2:9; Acts 1:9).

The Hebrew word in the Old Testament that is translated 'glory' (*kabod*) originally expressed the idea of *weight*. From this it came to mean that which makes a person weighty in the eyes of others, and leads them to honour and respect him. Accordingly, Jacob's wealth and Joseph's prosperity are called 'glory' (Gen. 31:1, KJV; 45:13). Then the word was extended to mean honour and respect itself. Both ideas are conveyed in 2 Corinthians 4:17, 'For our light affliction, which is but for a moment, is working for us a far more exceeding and eternal weight of glory.' Or, if you like, the worth of gold is weighed in carats, and the more carats a gold coin weighs, the greater is its value. In Biblical terms, God's glory is the limitless superlative quality of His divine nature.

The second sense in which God's glory is spoken of in Scripture may be called His *ascriptive* glory or honour: 'Give unto the LORD the glory due to His name; worship the LORD in the beauty of holiness' (Ps. 29:2). God's glory involves a two-sided relationship. He is a God who reveals His glory, and His creatures, men and angels, respond by ascribing to Him the glory or honour due to His name (1 Chron. 16:28-29; Ps. 29:2; 1 Cor. 6:20). There is a glory that belongs intrinsically to God, and there is a glory that is due to God. This glory is the worship and praise, the love and service which His creatures give God in response to what He has shown them of Himself. The term 'glory' thus connects the thoughts of God's praiseworthiness and of His praise which is the right response when we realise that God stands before us, and we before Him. To quote J.I. Packer, 'The to-and-fro of seeing glory in God and giving glory to God is the true fulfillment of human nature at its heart, and it brings supreme joy to man just as it does to God (Zeph. 3:14-17).'[1]

THE GLORY OF GOD REVEALED

God's glory is revealed in *creation* by His power: 'The heavens declare the glory of God; and the firmament shows His handiwork' (Ps. 19:1); and 'For since the creation of the world His invisible attributes are clearly seen, being understood by the things that are made, even His eternal power and Godhead, so that they [human beings] are without excuse, because, although they knew God, they did not glorify Him as God, nor were thankful, but became futile in their thoughts, and their foolish hearts were darkened. Professing to be wise, they became fools, and changed the glory of the incorruptible God into an image made like corruptible man—and birds and four-footed animals and creeping things' (Rom. 1:20-23).

---

1. J.I. Packer, *Concise Theology*, p.59.

God's glory is also revealed in *providence* by His justice and goodness and sovereignty displayed in history. For example, His destruction of the world by means of a flood (Gen. 6-8); or the confusion of languages at the tower of Babel (Gen. 11:1-9); or the crossings of the Red Sea and the River Jordan in full flood by the Israelites (Exod. 14; Josh. 2), to name just a few of the many divine interventions recorded in Scripture by which God revealed His glory to men.

God's glory, however, is supremely revealed in *redemption* by His grace (2 Cor. 4:6; Heb. 1:3); that is to say, by the sending of His only Son, Jesus Christ, to save hell-deserving sinners. Scripture clearly points this out at every significant stage of our Lord's life and ministry: His incarnation (John 1:14); His miracles (John 2:11); His transfiguration (2 Pet. 1:17); His death (John 12:23-24; 13:31); His resurrection (Rom. 6:4); and His second coming (2 Thess. 1:10).

HOW GOD'S GLORY IS BEING RESTORED ON EARTH

God's goal on earth is to fully restore His ascriptive glory. The grand purpose of God is to fulfil the prayer Jesus taught us to pray: 'Our Father in heaven, hallowed be Your name. Your kingdom come. Your will be done on earth as it is in heaven' (Matt. 6:9-10); in other words, to reverse the effects of the fall of man into sin and humble his pride before the greatness and goodness of his Maker. The essence of all sin is pride, for it was pride that led the devil to think that he had a right to the worship of his fellow angels. So in his arrogance he made a grab for the throne of heaven, and was promptly expelled with the angels who rebelled with him (Jude 6). In an act of further rebellion, the devil enticed Adam and Eve to disobey God by appealing to their pride as well. 'You will not surely die' if you eat of the fruit which God has forbidden, he said, 'for God knows that in the day you eat of it ... you will be like God' (Gen. 3:4-5). It was pride and self-importance that made our first parents disobey God and bring the curse of sin on earth and all mankind.

Pride is still the prime cause of sin, because sin continually seeks to dethrone God in order to serve self. Even when we become Christians, pride remains a thorn in our flesh. It was a serious problem in the church Paul founded at Corinth, where some were glorying in men, saying, 'I am of Paul' or 'I am of Apollos' or 'I am of Cephas.' In response the apostle asked: 'Is Christ divided? Was Paul crucified for you? Or were you baptized in the name of Paul?' (1 Cor. 1:12-13). He concludes his reasoning by saying, 'For you see your calling, brethren, that not many wise according to the flesh, not many mighty, not many noble, are called. But God has chosen the foolish things of the world to put to shame the wise, and God has chosen the weak things of the world to put to shame the things which are mighty; and the base things of the world and the things which are despised God has chosen, and the things which are not, to bring to nothing the things that are, that no flesh should glory in His presence ... that, as it is written, "He who glories, let him glory in the LORD"' (1:26-29,31). The church at Corinth was full of pride over position, gifts and knowledge, and it grieved Paul greatly. It comes up again in chapter 3:21, 'Let no one glory in men,' and again in chapter 10:31, 'Whatever you do, do all to the glory of God.'

God the Creator rules His world for His glory. He does not exist for our sake, but we for His. It is the nature and prerogative of God to please Himself, and Scripture tells us that it is His good pleasure to exalt Himself in our eyes: 'Be still, and know that I am God;

I will be exalted among the nations, I will be exalted in the earth!' (Ps. 46:10). God's supreme goal is to glorify Himself. It was for this that God decreed to create the world and everything in it. And it was for this that He willed to permit sin. He could have created men and angels incapable of sinning, but He did not. Why? For His own glory; for there is nothing so glorious in God as His unsolicited, unmerited grace revealed in the atoning death of His only Son on behalf of His penitent, believing people. God was not bound to take action to save us. His resolve to give His Son as a sacrifice for sinners was a free choice which He need never have made. Why did it please Him to love and redeem the unlovely and the undeserving? Paul tells us three times in one chapter that God did it 'to the praise of the glory of His grace', or 'the praise of His glory' (Eph. 1:6,12,14).

God's glory is restored by the humbling of proud sinners
God's purpose in working in the world is to ensure 'that no flesh should glory in His presence' (1 Cor. 1:29). The Oxford Dictionary defines the verb *glory* as 'to exalt, to pride oneself in something'. It also means to put our trust in it and esteem it above all else. Sin has so dulled our sense of the excellence and supremacy of God, that we have become preoccupied with self-importance and self-esteem. We make idols of ourselves and regard our own temporal interests as supreme in spite of the fact that God's word says, '"Let not the wise man glory in his wisdom, let not the mighty man glory in his might, nor let the rich man glory in his riches; but let him who glories glory in this, that he understands and knows Me, that I am the LORD, exercising lovingkindness, judgment, and righteousness in the earth. For in these I delight," says the LORD' (Jer. 9:23-24).

The first commandment says that it is a sin to have any other gods besides Jehovah, or to love and serve anything more than Him. For in doing that, we have 'exchanged the truth of God for the lie [the lie that God is dispensable] and worshiped and served the creature rather than the Creator, who is blessed forever. Amen' (Rom. 1:25). Pride has poisoned the entire life of every human being, and as a result, says Paul, 'the message of the cross is foolishness to those who are perishing, but to us who are being saved it is the power of God ... Where is the wise? ... Where is the disputer [the debater] of this age? Has not God made foolish the wisdom of this world?' (1 Cor. 1:18-21). It is God's purpose by the preaching of the gospel (the message of the cross) to save us from the eternal destruction that the proud wisdom of man has brought upon the world. In response, 'Jews request a sign, and Greeks seek after wisdom; but we preach Christ crucified, to the Jews a stumbling block and to the Greeks foolishness' (1 Cor. 1:22-23).

Why was the message of Christ crucified 'a stumbling block to the Jews'? The answer, quite simply, is pride. They 'trusted in themselves that they were righteous, and despised others' (Luke 18:9). Like Saul of Tarsus, they were religious people who sought to live by the Ten Commandments and establish a righteousness of their own before God (Phil. 3:4-10). Naturally, when they heard the gospel preached and were told that 'there is none who does good, no, not one ... for all have sinned and fall short of the glory of God' (Rom. 3:12,23), they were indignant. They were even more infuriated to hear that the Messiah they had crucified had to die on the cross to atone for their sins and provide righteousness as a free gift to be received by faith (Rom. 3:21-26). The preaching of 'Christ crucified' stripped them of all their religious works, and therefore was 'a stumbling block' (lit. an offence) to them. That is still true of all religious people. Humility before God is by nature impossible. The only people who know they have no righteousness of their own, are those whose eyes have been opened by 'the power of God' and the message of 'Christ crucified'. For this purpose our Lord sent the Holy Spirit to 'convict the world of sin, righteousness and judgment' (John 16:8-11).

If the message of Christ crucified was an 'offence' to the Jews, why was it 'foolishness' to the Greeks? The answer again is pride, for the Greeks (as representatives of the Gentiles) prided themselves in their 'wisdom' (v. 22). In the four hundred years leading up to Jesus Christ, Greece produced the greatest thinkers in history. Socrates, Plato and Aristotle are still admired for their wisdom. The Greeks, therefore, put their confidence in their rational powers, and put to the test of reason the gospel was sheer 'foolishness'. Why would a God who created heaven and earth want to become a man and live in poverty? And why would He allow Himself to be crucified when He had the power to destroy His enemies? And if He rose again from the dead and returned to the heavens, how could He save the world from all its evils? The gospel makes no sense to the worldly wise.

So Paul has to remind the Greeks in Corinth that human wisdom cannot be relied on because it has been affected by sin. What they dismiss as 'the foolishness of God', is 'wiser than men'. Only the convincing power of the Holy Spirit can deliver men from the folly and ignorance of trusting in human wisdom to understand the things of God. Thus Paul says in chapter 2:4, 'My speech and my preaching were not with persuasive words of human wisdom, but in demonstration of the

Spirit and of power, that your faith should not be in the wisdom of men, but in the power of God.' Before we come to Christ our trust is firmly placed in our own sinful and corrupted ability to discover the truth. But when by the grace and power of God we are brought to faith in Jesus Christ, we see that the wisdom we trusted in is foolishness of the worst kind; foolishness that damns a soul to hell (John 3:16-31). And why does God display His saving power through the gospel of Christ crucified in this way? Paul says God does it 'that no flesh should glory in His presence'. He does it to humble us. The whole world is divided into these two groups: the proud and the humble; between those who trust in themselves and those who are 'poor in spirit' (Matt. 5:3).

God's glory is restored by the saving of helpless sinners
Paul describes the process of salvation in 1 Corinthians 1:30, 'But of Him you are in Christ Jesus, who became for us wisdom from God—and righteousness and sanctification and redemption.' Salvation is something much more than a mental assent to the wisdom of God in the gospel. God must actually do something supernatural in our lives before we will stop boasting of ourselves and start glorying only in the Lord. 'But of Him [of God] you are in Christ Jesus.' Christians have been miraculously united in their spirit to Jesus Christ by faith, and just as a branch draws its life from the vine to which it is united, so the Christian draws his spiritual life from the Spirit of Christ to whom God has united him (John 15:1-5). It is all of God! So the tendency of the Corinthians to glory in their allegiance to Paul or Apollos or Peter was worldly and sinful. They had received nothing from men. Without the power of God these preachers would have laboured in vain. As

Paul says in chapter 3:6, 'I planted, Apollos watered, but God gave the increase.'

In the salvation of sinners, as in everything else, it is God's will that 'no flesh should glory in His presence' (that is, in His sight) In chapter 6 Paul tells us that before their conversion the Corinthians had been fornicators, idolaters, adulterers, homosexuals, sodomites, thieves, drunkards and revilers, among other evils (vv. 9-11). It was the power of God that had taken hold of these sinners and radically transformed them. In chapter 4:7 Paul asks, 'What do you have that you did not receive? Now if you did indeed receive it, why do you boast as if you had not received it?' It is God who is to be praised for the gift of salvation. In Matthew 11:25-26, when our Lord compares His disciples with the people of Capernaum who did not believe in Him in spite of the mighty works He did among them, He prays: 'I thank You, Father, Lord of heaven and earth, that You have hidden these things from the wise and the prudent and revealed them to babes. Even so, Father, for so it seemed good in Your sight.' That is the Christian's attitude. We never praise people for becoming Christians. Whenever we hear of a person's conversion, it is God who is to be thanked and glorified. 'Of Him you are in Christ Jesus.' That is the origin of the Christian life. 'Salvation is of the LORD' (Jonah 2:9).

What then is salvation? What does God do for us when we come to Christ in faith and are united to Him? Paul's answer is 'Of Him you are in Christ Jesus, who became for us wisdom from God – and righteousness, and sanctification and redemption.' Those four blessings cover our main spiritual needs. The needs of our soul are great indeed, and the first in order, as we have already seen, is 'wisdom.' Our minds have been darkened by sin, and our ignorance of the living and true God needs to be dispelled. We desperately need to learn who God really is and what He has done to save us from sin and eternal death. We need 'the fear of God which is the beginning of wisdom' (Ps. 111:10). That is what Paul means when he says that Christ 'became for us wisdom from God'. Christ Jesus came to earth as God incarnate to show us by His life, words and deeds what God is like, and how God can save us. Jesus came to be the spiritual 'light of the world', and said, 'He who follows Me shall not walk in darkness, but have the light of life' (John 8:12). To follow Jesus, is to obey His teaching in the New Testament and we can only do this through the Holy Spirit whom He has given to be our indwelling Helper (John 16:13-15).

The next three nouns in verse 30 are Paul's amplification of the wisdom Christ has become for us. In the first place, it is wisdom to make us 'righteous' before God. For we are transgressors who have deeply offended God and desperately need to be put in the right with Him. The penalty of sin which is death and hell needs to be paid. God's law and God's justice need to be satisfied before we can be forgiven and reconciled to God. This is precisely what God did for us in Christ's atoning death on the cross. To quote Paul, 'He made Him who knew no sin to be sin for us, that we might become the righteousness of God in Him;' and 'Christ died for our sins according to the Scriptures' (2 Cor. 5:21; 1 Cor. 15:3). His death was a double exchange for all believers. We receive His righteousness in exchange for our sin.

In the second place, the wisdom Christ has become for us is seen as well in the fact that by His death and resurrection He has also provided 'sanctification' or holiness for us. We need something more than forgiveness and reconciliation, for our hearts are totally depraved and prone to evil. We need to be made pure from within, and in order to do that, Christ sent His Spirit to dwell in us not only as our *teacher*, but also as our *sanctifier*. He has divine power to regenerate us, giving us holy desires and the ability to carry them out. He gives us a growing love for God, His word, His people and good deeds (Rom. 8:1-2; Titus 2:11-14).

In the third place, the wisdom of God is seen in the fact that in Christ He has made provision for 'redemption'. The consummation of our salvation is going to result in 'the redemption of our body' (Rom. 8:23). Death is not going to have the last word. God has done this so that 'no flesh should glory in His presence', but that the Scripture might be fulfilled which says: 'He who glories, let him glory in the LORD' (1 Cor. 1:29,31).

Pride (literally, haughty eyes) takes first place among the seven things in Proverbs 6:16-19 that God hates most. The purpose of the gospel, therefore, is not just to save our souls from hell and make us happy, but to bring glory to God. God's goal on earth is the restoration of His ascriptive glory, and because God is God this end is assured. As Augustus H. Strong comments, 'God will get glory out of every human life. Man may glorify God voluntarily by love and obedience, but if he will not do this he will be compelled to glorify God by his rejection and punishment.'[2]

J.I. Packer sums this subject up well when he writes:

God would not share with idols [the gods of Cyrus] the praise for restoring His people [to Jerusalem and their homeland], for idols, being unreal, contributed nothing to this work of grace (Isa. 42:8; 48:11); and God will not share the praise for salvation with its

2. Augustus H. Strong, quoted by John Blanchard, *More Gathered Gold* (Evangelical Press, 1986), p. 111.

human subjects today, for we too contribute nothing more to it than our need of it. First to last, and at every stage in the process, salvation comes from the Lord, and our praise must show our awareness of that. This is why Reformation theology was so insistent on the principle, 'Glory to God *alone*' (*soli Deo gloria*), and why we need to maintain that principle with equal zeal today.[3]

We will, if we are truly godly men and women. For godliness is the quality of life which exists in those who seek to glorify God. A godly person's ambition is to carry out the great principle in which Paul summed up the practice of Christianity: 'Glorify God in your body and in your spirit which are God's'; 'whether you eat or drink, or whatever you do, do all to the glory of God' (1 Cor. 6:20; 10:31). A godly person's dearest wish is to exalt God with all that he is and in all that he does. He follows in the footsteps of his Lord and Saviour who could say at the end of his life here: 'I have glorified You on earth' (John 17:4). His attitude is also that of George Whitefield who said: 'Let the name of Whitefield perish, so long as God is glorified.' By this God knows His people and by this we may know we are His people.

---

3. J.I. Packer, *ibid*, pp. 60-61.

Grace
Publications

Grace Publications Trust

Grace Publications Trust is a not-for-profit organisation that exists to glorify God by making the truth of God's Word (as declared in the Baptist Confessions of 1689 and 1966) clear and understandable, so that:

- Christians will be helped to preach Christ
- Christians will know Christ better and delight in Him more
- Christians will be equipped to live for Christ
- Seekers will come to know Christ

From its beginning in the late 1970s the Trust has published simplified and modernised versions of important Christian books written earlier, for example by some of the Reformers and Puritans. These books have helped introduce the riches of the past to a new generation and have proved particularly useful in parts of Asia and Africa where English is widely spoken as a second language. These books are now appearing in editions co-published with Christian Focus as *Grace Essentials*.

More details of the Trust's work can be found on the web site at *www.gracepublications.co.uk*.

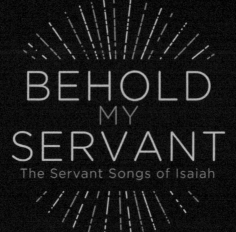

BEHOLD
MY
SERVANT
The Servant Songs of Isaiah

BRIAN A. RUSSELL

Behold My Servant
The Servant Songs of Isaiah
Brian A. Russell

- Isaiah 42-53
- An in-depth, exegetical devotional
- Discover Jehovah revealed as 'My Servant'

The Servant Songs of Isaiah are a beautiful topic for a devotional. Set in the context of Israel's failure, few places in the Old Testament speak so clearly about the merciful Messiah. To quote Henri Blocher, 'In them our Savour found the blueprint of His mission. From them Jesus learned that He would have to suffer for us; that He would die for us, as though He were a criminal, under the weight of our sins. How holy the ground we tread when studying the songs!'

ISBN: 978-1-78191-890-6

ASPECTS
of LOVE

OUR MAKER'S DESIGN FOR FRIENDSHIP,
LOVE, MARRIAGE AND FAMILY

WILLIAM J. U. PHILIP

Aspects of Love

Our Maker's design for friendship, love, marriage and family

William Philip

- Looks at love in various forms – friendship, marriage, family
- An antidote to the loneliness epidemic
- Affirms that all people are designed to love

We all want, and need, to love and to be loved. We are made in the image of God, who is love. Healthy loving is at the very heart of true human flourishing, but human life is full of love gone wrong – marriages break down, relationships with family members are strained, loneliness is an ever–increasing problem. This book delves into what the Bible has to say on relationships – friendship, love, marriage, sex and family – and how to guard them and keep them.

ISBN: 978-1-5271-0338-2

LEE GATISS

Light
after
Darkness

HOW THE REFORMERS
REGAINED, RETOLD AND RELIED
ON THE GOSPEL OF GRACE

Light after Darkness

How the Reformers regained, retold and relied
on the gospel of grace
Lee Gatiss

- The stories of 5 prominent Reformers
- Issues addressed by each Reformer
- Short, easy to read introduction to crucial church history

The Protestant Reformers of the sixteenth century regained, retold, and relied on the gospel of grace — and we can learn from their tragedies and triumphs, their dark deeds and noble heroics. The stories of Ulrich Zwingli, William Tyndale, Martin Luther, John Calvin and Thomas Cranmer remind us of the glorious truths which warmed the hearts and fired the souls of passionate and imperfect people, and how they tried to share the good news of Jesus Christ in their generation. Will it strengthen and inspire passionate and imperfect Christians today to emulate their clarity, their courage, and their compassion for the lost?

ISBN: 978-1-5271-0333-7

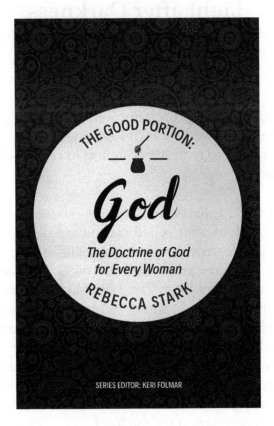

THE GOOD PORTION:

God

The Doctrine of God
for Every Woman

REBECCA STARK

SERIES EDITOR: KERI FOLMAR

Good Portion – God

The Doctrine of God for Every Woman

Rebecca Stark

- A Biblical look at the Character and Person of God
- Thematic, easy to read chapters
- Can be used for personal devotions or group study
- Second title in a ten–part doctrine series

God has revealed Himself to us in His Word. As we study what He says about Himself, and see more of His perfection, worth, magnificence and beauty, we glimpse His glory. This second title in *The Good Portion* series looks at what the Bible says about God – Father, Son and Holy Spirit – that we might know Him better and glorify Him.

ISBN: 978-1-5271-0111-1

Christian Focus Publications

Our mission statement —

STAYING FAITHFUL

In dependence upon God we seek to impact the world through literature faithful to His infallible Word, the Bible. Our aim is to ensure that the Lord Jesus Christ is presented as the only hope to obtain forgiveness of sin, live a useful life and look forward to heaven with Him.

Our books are published in four imprints:

CHRISTIAN
FOCUS

Popular works including biographies, commentaries, basic doctrine and Christian living.

CHRISTIAN
HERITAGE

Books representing some of the best material from the rich heritage of the church.

MENTOR

Books written at a level suitable for Bible College and seminary students, pastors, and other serious readers. The imprint includes commentaries, doctrinal studies, examination of current issues and church history.

CF4•K

Children's books for quality Bible teaching and for all age groups: Sunday school curriculum, puzzle and activity books; personal and family devotional titles, biographies and inspirational stories — because you are never too young to know Jesus!

Christian Focus Publications Ltd,
Geanies House, Fearn, Ross-shire,
IV20 1TW, Scotland, United Kingdom.
www.christianfocus.com
blog.christianfocus.com